More Science Through Children's Literature

MORE SCIENCE THROUGH CHILDREN'S LITERATURE

An Integrated Approach

Carol M. Butzow
Educational Consultant

and

John W. Butzow
Dean, College of Education
Indiana University of Pennsylvania

Illustrated by
Rhett E. Kennedy

1998
TEACHER IDEAS PRESS
A Division of
Libraries Unlimited, Inc.
Englewood, Colorado

To our parents, E. H., J. B., and E. B.

TEACHER IDEAS PRESS
A Division of
Libraries Unlimited, Inc.
P.O. Box 6633
Englewood, CO 80155-6633
1-800-237-6124
www.lu.com/tip

Production Editor: Kay Mariea
Copy Editor: Jason Cook
Proofreader: Louise Tonneson
Indexer: Christine Smith
Layout: Pamela J. Getchell

Library of Congress Cataloging-in-Publication Data

Butzow, Carol M., 1942-
    More science through children's literature : an integrated
approach / Carol M. Butzow and John W. Butzow ; illustrated by Rhett
E. Kennedy.
    xviii, 245 p. 22x28 cm.
    Includes bibliographical references and index.
    ISBN 1-56308-266-7
    1. Science--Study and teaching (Elementary)   2. Education,
Elementary--Activity programs.   3. Children--Books and reading.
4. Children's literature.   I. Butzow, John W., 1939-   .
II. Kennedy, Rhett E.   III. Title.
LB1585.B843   1998
372.3'5044--dc21   98-2734
                                                       CIP

Contents

Part I—Life Science

Part II—Earth and Space Sciences

Preface

No top-down mandate can replace the insights and skills teachers need to manage complex classrooms and address the different needs of individual students, whatever their age. No textbook, packaged curriculum, or testing system can discern what students already know or create the rich array of experiences they need to move ahead. . . . When all is said and done, if students are to be well taught, it will be done by knowledgeable and well-supported teachers.

—National Commission on Teaching and America's Future[1]

More Science Through Children's Literature, as well as the other books we have written—*Science Through Children's Literature* and *Intermediate Science Through Children's Literature*—have been based on the belief that the teacher is the most important element in teaching children. Our purpose has been to offer ideas, activities, and resources to assist teachers in making the important day-by-day decisions necessary to help all learners reach a fuller understanding of science, its nature and content. Our integrated units are more than just collections of facts and recipes to be followed; they are resources upon which to build interdisciplinary lessons that will accommodate the needs of all children.

Our two previous books were well received by teachers. Many teachers who attended our presentations asked us when we would produce additional materials for teachers of K–3 children. *More Science Through Children's Literature* is the result of four years of extensive work reviewing many books to select literature to form the basis of a follow-up work.

This book includes 21 chapters, each built around a work of fictional children's literature. The literature is not merely a place to begin when introducing a unit of activities, nor is it merely a summation of the activities. These books were selected because they offer a wealth of information about topics that are worth considerable activity, thought, and reflection. We have selected books with strong scientific themes—themes that can become the basis of scientific activities, as well as activities in related areas, such as social studies, humanities, arts, and mathematics. This creates a unit of instruction that is truly interdisciplinary in nature. A clear sign that integration is working is when it becomes impossible to discern what subject is being taught.

Children's literature provides engaging story lines that children can easily understand and effortlessly remember, especially when compared to the stream of facts typical in expository text. From their understanding and memory, children are able to formulate relationships between the subject matter and the real world. The narrative glues together the pieces of fact and presents them at a level of accessibility that is appropriate for the child.

Following this preface is an introduction that discusses the definition of science and the integrated science instruction we advocate. The units of study are divided into three parts: "Life Science," which includes studies of individual life-forms, as well as the ecology of plants and animals; "Earth and Space Sciences," which includes studies of weather, soil and rocks, the planet Earth, the solar system, and the universe; and "Physical Science and Technology," which includes studies of force, work, energy, sound, music, wind, and flight.

Our suggestion for using these units of study includes reading (and rereading) the entire children's literature book aloud to the class or with the class. For many units, we suggest a prereading activity for children or the teacher that should be completed before beginning the unit to make possible a fuller use of the content of the focal story. This activity might include ordering materials from a vendor, locating pictures and maps, or downloading sound files from the Internet. In other cases, it is an activity that will allow children to better appreciate the story. For example, in *Katy and the Big Snow*, we suggest using related books by Virginia Lee Burton to examine the role of machines. Once the unit is begun, the activities can be followed in any manner or order, based on the particular group of students. A unit of study may be quite different in content and presentation with each group of children.

We have chosen to examine intensely a few works of children's literature, rather than compile an exhaustive annotated bibliography of possible science-related books for children. The literature selected fulfills two basic requirements: It must tell a good story, and it must contain strong scientific themes that can be easily integrated with the other subjects in the curriculum. We suggest concepts and activities that may be used by teachers, librarians, and youth-group leaders, or in a home-schooling environment, while working with individuals or groups of children.

We understand the difference between the resource style of our writing and lesson plans. Teachers should use suggested activities in the framework of their own lesson plans. They should select appropriate activities and plan accordingly. A unit is not a list of activities that must be presented in a specific order, nor is it feasible that every activity could be presented during a unit of instruction. In a very few cases, a particular order must be followed to make sense of certain activities, but generally, they can be carried out in the order that best fits the teaching style and learning styles of the classroom. The building-block essentials of each unit have been provided, but a unit can come to fruition only when applied to a particular class of children.

Notes

1. National Commission on Teaching and America's Future, *What Matters Most: Teaching for America's Future* (New York: Teachers College, Columbia University, 1996), 10.

Related Books and References

Butzow, Carol M. *A Comparison of a Storyline Based Method of Instruction and a Textbook Method of Instruction on the Acquisition of Science Concepts in the Elementary School.* Dissertation submitted to the Graduate School, Indiana University of Pennsylvania, 1991, in partial fulfillment of the requirements for an Ed.D.

Butzow, Carol M., and John W. Butzow. *Intermediate Science Through Children's Literature: Over Land and Sea.* Englewood, CO: Teacher Ideas Press, 1994.

———. *Science Through Children's Literature: An Integrated Approach.* Englewood, CO: Teacher Ideas Press, 1989.

Acknowledgments

To Professor James Dearing of the Indiana University of Pennsylvania Music Department, for suggesting music appropriate to the units of instruction.

To the Northern New England Marine Education Project of the University of Maine—University of New Hampshire Sea Grant Program, for ideas on freshwater and saltwater activities and resources.

To Adam Buchanan, for making many paper airplanes.

To our daughters, Karen and Kristen, for asking, "How is the book coming?"

Introduction

Since the publication of our first book, *Science Through Children's Literature*, in 1989, three major events have influenced the role of science education in the school: 1) the emergence of scientific literacy as the major goal of teaching science to elementary school children; 2) the commissioning of standards for teaching and learning science; and 3) the acknowledgment that teacher empowerment is the keystone to school reform.

Another change that has occurred in the last few years is a modification of the definition of science, previously defined as the content to be learned or the fields of specialization that are included in its study. Robert Yager and other science educators now espouse a much different definition: "Anything that promotes explanation, encourages the creation of explanations, or calls for verification and validation is science."[1] The view of science taken in this book is one that emphasizes the investigative nature of the endeavor and views broadly the contexts for investigation, as evidenced by the Yager definition.

If scientific literacy for everyone is the hallmark of achievement in science education, as defined above, then all learners must be allowed to develop their powers of observation and reasoning. In the past, it was acknowledged that science education should be guided by teacher demonstrations or individual, hands-on experiences, but the external validity of what children learned and the terms used to describe it were of more concern than the processes learned by the individual child. The significant change in scientific literacy today is a much greater emphasis on what children learn to do, rather than on what they appear to know.

A scientifically literate person is someone who is willing to examine a situation in detail and assemble and test explanations for what is happening. Scientific literacy is not achieved by the acquisition of facts, but rather by the use of reasoning and observation to reach plausible conclusions. The scientifically literate person is intuitive, curious, and open-minded. To foster the development of creative problem-solvers, schools must provide a suitable environment.

How does science education foster the achievement of scientific literacy? It does this by supporting, cherishing, and nurturing the natural curiosity that children exhibit. We believe that children's literature can be used to keep alive this sense of wonder and can become a vehicle through which science is learned. In this book, we have selected works of children's literature that are aimed at eliciting children's imaginative powers. At the same time, we have suggested activities to assist them in developing reasoning skills and integrating areas of the curriculum.

The goal of science education should not be the memorization of how phenomena occur. Rather, the goal should be for all children to construct concepts themselves. For example, in Chapter 21, "Airplanes and Flight" (constructed around the book *Plane Song* by Diane Siebert), is an activity in which children follow directions to make a paper airplane and then observe how it flies. After this, children are asked to improve the design of the paper airplane. An advocacy of having children work directly with materials to create, or construct, a personal set of ideas is called constructivism. In practice, the teacher who uses constructivism as a guide considers the use of the child's background and ability to interpret new experiences and ideas. This teacher knows that ideas grow more from what is inside the child than what is outside and, hence, uses the familiar and ordinary to assist children in constructing their own concepts.

The commissioning of standards was motivated by a desire to provide high-quality science education for all children. The new standards emphasize the development of scientific literacy. Standards have been published by the National Science Teachers Association, Project 2061 of the American Association for the Advancement of Science, and more recently, by the National Research Council. The National Research Council's recent book *National Science Education Teaching Standards* includes a chapter devoted to standards for teaching science. The assumptions behind these standards for teaching science include the following:

Student understanding is actively constructed through individual and social processes.

What students learn is greatly influenced by how they are taught.

The actions of teachers are deeply influenced by their perceptions of science as an enterprise and as a subject to be taught and learned.

Actions of teachers are deeply influenced by their understanding of and relationships with students.

The job of the teacher is to help children achieve independent investigation. Children are assisted in determining what and how to investigate. This vision of science education requires that the teacher help children relate to what is to be learned, on their own terms, and then help children focus their imagination on how to construct meaning. The new standards empower teachers to be curriculum leaders. The teacher has more ownership over lessons and freedom from applying predeveloped lessons from published curricula.

Given that science should be taught by an empowered teacher for the development of scientific literacy, how does science relate to children's literature? Our answer is that, early in life, children are not as capable of logical thought as mature adults. They are, however, quite capable of appreciating a good story. The story line provides its own logic in uniting the elements of the story. Excellent works of children's literature relate scientific concepts in superb story lines that hold the elements of the story together like a strong glue. The narrative of the story assists young learners in developing knowledge and comprehension before children are capable of applying adult logic.

In the book *Berlioz the Bear* by Jan Brett (the focal book of Chapter 16, "Force, Motion, and Music"), a challenge is presented: how to free a large wagon full of musicians from a pothole in the road. Many solutions are attempted, as suggested by passing onlookers. Animals of various shapes and sizes try to pull the wagon out of its predicament but fail one after another. Finally, a bee stings the mule, who suddenly "accelerates" the wagon and frees it from the hole. The musicians are then able to reach their concert in the nick of time. With this background, children are able to develop their concepts of force and motion.

Berlioz the Bear has a persistent theme related to science, but this theme is not expressed in scientific terminology. The problem of moving a wagon is the focus of this interesting story. The setting is somewhere in central Europe, probably during the mid-nineteenth century. The book is lavishly illustrated to show a folk festival in action. The wagon is festooned with flowers; the characters are depicted in ethnic costumes; and the village seems to erupt with life. The characters are "animal people," who demonstrate human characteristics while retaining fantasy attributes. The plot—the musicians trying to get to town to play in the festival—unfolds, but with a surprise ending when the mule responds to an unexpected stimulus.

For our third "volume" of *Science Through Children's Literature*, we have selected 21 books that have the strong characteristics of the previous example: persistent scientific theme, an inviting setting, clear characterization, and a well-developed and convincing plot. The scientific content is not merely a chance to introduce a reading. It becomes a "character" in the story, without which the book would cease to exist. These are not treatises on science, but good stories, waiting to engage the imaginative powers of children and teachers, alike.

Our books, *Science Through Children's Literature*, *Intermediate Science Through Children's Literature*, and *More Science Through Children's Literature*, were written to give teachers a choice of activities to use as they create lesson plans. We have selected books rich in content that can be "experienced" by children through a variety of hands-on activities and other active means, such as choral reading or inventing new endings to the story. Our approach has been to select books that naturally provide science content for children to explore. When subject areas other than science emerge from these stories, we have considered them appropriate for inclusion, emphasizing a natural, flexible integration in the activities.

The implications of scientific literacy, commissioning of standards, and empowerment of teachers are exerting an influence on today's elementary curriculum. In applying these influences to the teaching of science, we have adapted these comparisons from the National Research Council's standards document:

More Emphasis	**Less Emphasis**
Individual and group interests	Everyone must learn the same things in the same way
The curriculum is selected based on locale and individual needs	The curriculum is the same everywhere, for everyone
Children actively inquire	Children learn what the teacher presents
Explanations are developed and defended by learners	Explanations are recited
Assessment is based on what is done	Assessment is based on tests that cover factual information
The classroom is a learning community	Individual competition is fostered
Teachers work cooperatively with specialists, including library media specialists	Teachers work individually

As you use these units of study in your classroom, we encourage you to consider our suggested activities as guides for fostering active, creative expression in children. In your quest for the advancement of scientific literacy, and the implementation of the national science teaching standards, we hope that these units will motivate you to take a more active approach to teaching science—by using children's literature in an integrated curriculum.

Notes

1. Robert Yager, John McClure, and Jeffrey Weld, "Applying Science Across the Curriculum," *Educational Leadership* 50 (May 1993): 79.

Related Books and References

Brett, Jan. *Berlioz the Bear*. New York: G. P. Putnam's Sons, 1991.

National Research Council. "Science Teaching Standards." Chap. 3 in *National Science Education Teaching Standards*. Washington, DC: National Academy Press, 1996.

Siebert, Diane. *Plane Song*. New York: HarperCollins, 1993.

Part I
Life Science

Chapter 1

Arctic Animals

Here Is the Arctic Winter

by Madeleine Dunphy
New York: Hyperion Books for Children, 1993

Summary

The creatures of the Arctic live in a land of perpetual night. Each species struggles for survival in a hostile environment of predator-prey relationships.

Science and Content Related Concepts

Food chain, predator-prey relationships, climate, seasons, Arctic winter, survival

Content Related Words

Inuit, Arctic ice, protection, camouflage, northern lights (aurora borealis)

Activities

1. The Arctic Ocean surrounds the North Pole. Using a globe, have children find this ocean. What countries does it touch? Which states of the United States does it touch? Certain areas of this ocean that are closer to land are called seas. Have children locate these seas. Why is it better to use a globe than a flat projection map when studying this area?

2. *Here Is the Arctic Winter* is a story of the animals that survive in this severe environment. Divide the class into groups of two or three children each, and have each group select an animal from those shown on the last page of the book. Have each group research their animal and write a brief report, including the following information:

   Animal's name

   Description of the animal

   Size and weight of the animal

   Animals upon which it preys

   Animals that prey upon it

   Distinguishing characteristics of the animal

3. Protective adaptation is how an animal changes, over time, to better survive in its environment. Camouflage is an important part of this adaptation. In the Arctic winter, the predominant background color is white. Many Arctic animals, too, are colored white, an adaptation that protects them from being seen. Cut out white silhouettes of the animals shown in this book (see fig. 1.1) and hide them around the classroom. Have children identify the places where the animals are most effectively hidden. Which places are dangerous for a white-colored animal that must hide from predators?

4. The black of the Arctic winter and the white of the animals and the ice make for a scenario of little color. This helps animals to camouflage themselves for protection. Ask children what life would be like if their environment had little color. Hold an "Arctic Winter Day": Have everyone wear black and white, and mute the colors of the classroom—use black and white construction paper to mask bookshelves and tops of desks. White sheets may be hung to mask the walls.

5. To more concretely demonstrate how camouflage works, use a box of colored toothpicks (a variety of colors, including white and wood-colored toothpicks) and several pieces of cloth or paper (various colors) that can be used as backgrounds upon which to scatter the toothpicks. Scatter the toothpicks over a one-square-yard background. Ask a child to pick up as many toothpicks as possible, one at a time, in 10 seconds. Count the number of toothpicks of each color that have been retrieved. Continue the challenge, using the same background, with three or four more children, each time recording the counts. Change the background and repeat the activity. What colors of toothpicks are retrieved most frequently from each of the backgrounds? For each background, rank the colors, from the greatest number retrieved to the least number retrieved. From this activity, what can children conclude about the protective coloration of animals? NOTE: On a white background, white toothpicks should be retrieved least often, as these toothpicks will "hide" most effectively. This suggests, for example, that white animals of the Arctic would be best protected in that environment. The darker-colored toothpicks should be most effectively "protected" when scattered on a sheet of similarly colored cloth or paper.

6. Human beings do not appear in the story, yet they play an important role in the Arctic environment. What role do human beings play in the predator-prey relationships that occur in nature? To answer this question, it might help to know something about the Inuit culture. Ask a library media specialist to help children research the Inuit, or Eskimos, as they are sometimes called, answering such questions as: How does the Inuit culture differ from the non-Native American culture in regard to housing, clothing, food, transportation, and tools? Are human beings the predators, or are they preyed upon by the animals? How do the Inuit minimize their effect on the environment?

Fig. 1.1. Silhouettes of Arctic Animals.

From *More Science Through Children's Literature.* © 1998 Butzow and Butzow. Teacher Ideas Press. (800) 237-6124.

7. The Arctic environment is fragile and must be protected through wise use of resources. Unfortunately, resources are not always used wisely, and manufactured products are sometimes discarded carelessly. What happens to garbage in the Arctic environment? Under even the best circumstances, garbage decomposes slowly, but once garbage has been frozen, it literally will not decompose. To help children understand this process, have them try the following experiment (see fig. 1.2).

Fig. 1.2. Making a Decomposition Box.

a. Line two large, flat pans (with two-inch high sides) or garment-type boxes with large garbage bags.

b. Spread one inch of soil on the bottom of each pan or box. Cover this with a layer of garbage—newspapers, a tin can lid, aluminum foil, paper towels, wood shavings, plant leaves, bread, and potato peelings. Spread a layer of soil over the garbage.

c. Place one pan or box into a large freezer.

d. Water the other pan or box lightly every day for one month and let it sit at room temperature.

e. At the end of the month, have children examine the contents of both pans or boxes. Where has decomposition begun? What garbage has not decomposed and probably will not decompose or will do so slowly? What are the differences between the garbage that was frozen and the garbage that was left at room temperature? What can children conclude about "Arctic garbage?" How should trash and litter be disposed of in this environment? How might this trash affect the animals shown in the book?

8. Ask children to imagine what life would be like if they were visiting the Arctic during the days of perpetual darkness, November 18 through January 24. (Have them assume that they will be living in a town, such as Point Barrow, and attending school there.) Have them make a list of what they would need to have with them during this time. How would their lives be different? What things would be the same? What would they like about the differences? What would not be to their liking? Have children draw pictures of themselves living in the Arctic winter.

9. Animals play a significant role in the Inuit culture and are often the subject of their carvings (see fig. 1.3). These carvings are sculpted from a soft mineral called soapstone or talc. To simulate this Inuit art form, have children try carving a piece of soap using a small plastic knife. Other subjects of Inuit carvings are homes, people, and supernatural beings.

Fig. 1.3. Soap Stone Figures.

10. The Inuit have a strong tradition of oral storytelling—from simple stories of hunting and family life to tales of heroes who have supernatural powers or shamans with priestly powers. Also popular are stories about Raven, a trickster figure. Memorize an Inuit story to tell the children (e.g., "The Gift of the Whale" from *Keepers of the Animals* by Caduto and Bruchac). Have children write Inuit-type stories, practice reciting them aloud, and tell them to the group. NOTE: Ask a library media specialist for additional books about Native American folklore.

11. An important part of oral storytelling is visualizing the story as it is told. To help children develop their storytelling abilities, have them share their stories from activity 10 as plays, skits, pantomimes, or puppet shows.

12. To read further about the Inuit way of life, have children access the Internet at http://canada.gc.ca/canadiana/faitc/fa32.html or http://www.alaska.net/~nome/eculture.htm.

13. Insulation is important for all inhabitants of the Arctic, including people. Clothing and housing must be constructed with insulating qualities that help protect people from the cold. Have children, working alone or as a group, simulate the insulating qualities of various materials by finding a way to protect a two-inch cube of gelatin from the cold.

    a. Insert a thermometer into each of several two-inch cubes of gelatin.

    b. Wrap each cube of gelatin with a different insulating material (see fig. 1.4), or place it in a container and pack the insulating material around the gelatin. Use such materials as grass, Styrofoam, wool, and plastic wrap.

    c. Put the cubes into a freezer, or set them outside if doing this experiment during winter. Measure the temperature every 10 to 15 minutes, and record the numbers on a line graph. The warmer the gelatin remains, the better it has been insulated from the cold. Which materials have the best insulating qualities? Ask children how this relates to staying warm in the winter.

    d. Repeat the experiment to determine which material best insulates the gelatin from the heat. The cooler the gelatin remains, the better the gelatin has been insulated from the heat. Ask children how this relates to staying cool in the summer.

Fig. 1.4. Temperature Changes in Insulted Containers.

14. Children will enjoy playing a game of Concentration using cards that name the animals shown in this book (see fig. 1.5). Make two sets of cards for each pair of children. Place the cards face down in front of the children. The first child turns two cards face up. If the cards match, they are removed from play and the child scores one point. If the cards do not match, they are returned to the playing area, face down, and the second child takes a turn. (A child's turn continues until they fail to make a match.) The child with the most pairs is declared the winner. NOTE: To add a challenge to this game, require that children describe the animal before removing the pair of cards and scoring a point.

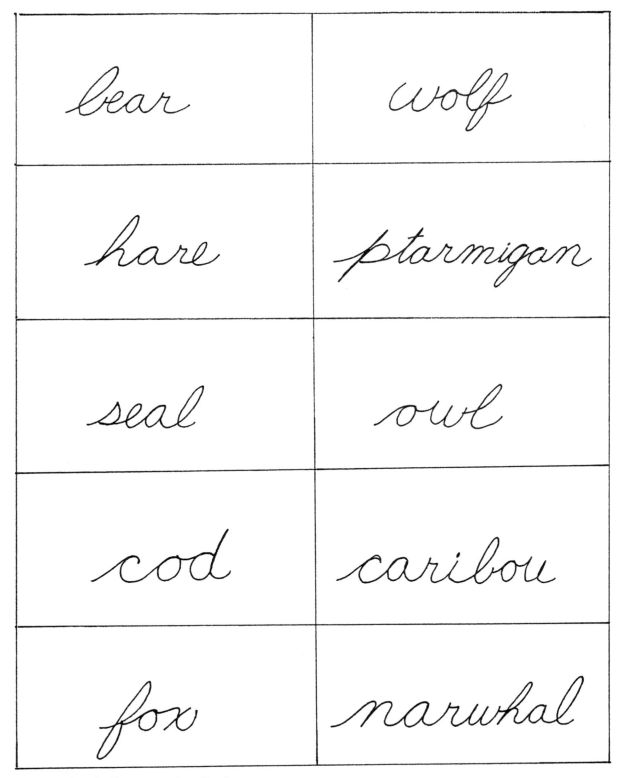

Fig. 1.5. Arctic Concentration Cards.

15. Math Puzzle—Arctic Animals
    Solve the arithmetic problems, then match the answers to the letter chart to decode the words. Correct answers will spell the names of the animals in *Here Is the Arctic Winter*.

A	B	C	D	E	F	G	H	I	J	K	L	M
1	2	3	4	5	6	7	8	9	10	11	12	13

N	O	P	Q	R	S	T	U	V	W	X	Y	Z
14	15	16	17	18	19	20	21	22	23	24	25	26

_____ _____ _____
5x3   20+3   8+4

_____ _____ _____ _____ _____ _____ _____
7x2   2-1   12+6   15+8   5-4   4x2   8+4

_____ _____ _____ _____ _____ _____ _____
2+1   1+0   9x2   3x3   1+1   20-5   7x3

_____ _____ _____
2x3   10+5   8x3

_____ _____ _____ _____ _____ _____ _____ _____ _____
4x4   25-5   8-7   12+6   7+6   3x3   4+3   1-0   10+4

_____ _____ _____ _____
16+7   8+7   15-3   8-2

_____ _____ _____ _____
6+2   8-7   12+6   2+3

_____ _____ _____
2+1   3x5   2x2

_____ _____ _____ _____
1+1   3+2   6-5   9+9

_____ _____ _____ _____
16+3   4+1   1+0   10+2

Related Books and References

Caduto, Michael J., and Joseph Bruchac. *Keepers of the Animals*. Golden, CO: Fulcrum Publishing, 1992.

De Larramendi, Ramon Hernando. "Perilous Journey: Three Years Across the Arctic." *National Geographic* 187, no. 1 (January 1995): 121–38.

Grove, Noel. "Alaska's Sky-High Wilderness." *National Geographic* 185, no. 5 (May 1994): 80–101.

Steger, Will. "Dispatches from the Arctic." *National Geographic* 189, no. 1 (January 1996): 78–89.

Vivaldi, Antonio. *The Four Seasons*. English Chamber Orchestra. Nigel Kennedy.

Chapter 2

Whales

Winter Whale

by Joanne Ryder
New York: Morrow Junior Books, 1991

Summary

This is the story of one of the largest creatures on Earth—the humpback whale. In the beginning of the book, a young boy walking in the rain assumes the identity of the whale. Throughout the book, he learns about the life of the whale, including eating, breaching, reproduction, communication, and migration. As the whale moves towards the shore, the boy reassumes his own identity, but he continues to ponder, in depth, the life of the whale.

Science and Content Related Concepts

Marine environment, oceans, whales

Content Related Words

Humpback whales, fluke, breaching, blowhole, dolphins, sea turtles

Activities

1. Humpback whales are typically about 50 feet long. To help the children understand the size of a humpback, make a life-size representation of this whale on a paved portion of the school playground or parking lot (see fig. 2.1a). Use a grid to enlarge a picture of a humpback (see fig. 2.1b). Mark the grid and the outline of the whale using chalk. Compare the length and height of the whale with objects that the children can visualize (e.g., the length of a car or school bus, the size of a baseball diamond, the size of the school gym or cafeteria, etc.). NOTE: If a grassy area is the only space available, use surveyor's tape to mark the grid and the outline of the whale.

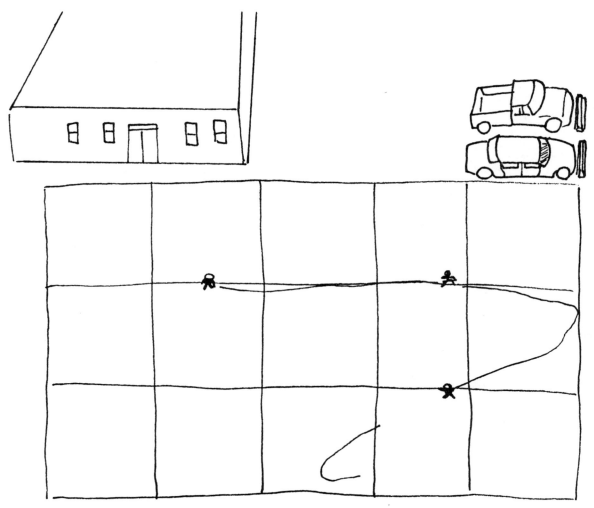

Fig. 2.1a. Parking Lot Whale.

2. Figure 2.2 shows whales in relative proportion to each other. Use this chart to discuss the different species of whales and their sizes when compared to each other, as well as to humans, elephants, and dinosaurs.

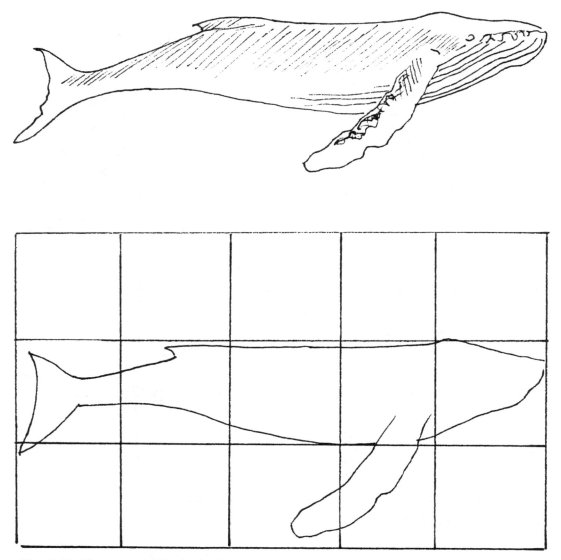

Fig. 2.1b. Humpback Whale Grid.

3. Using figure 2.2, have children sketch, color, or paint pictures of whales on posterboard. They should label the species of whales in their work. These pictures might be displayed as posters or as a diorama to decorate the room.

4. An extensive source of materials and information about whales is provided by WhaleNet. This endeavor was developed by Wheelock College and Simmons College faculty and students in Boston. These materials are available on the Internet at http://whale.simmons.edu. Pictures of a variety of whale species can also be found on the Internet at http://www.compusult.nf.ca/nfld/other/whales.

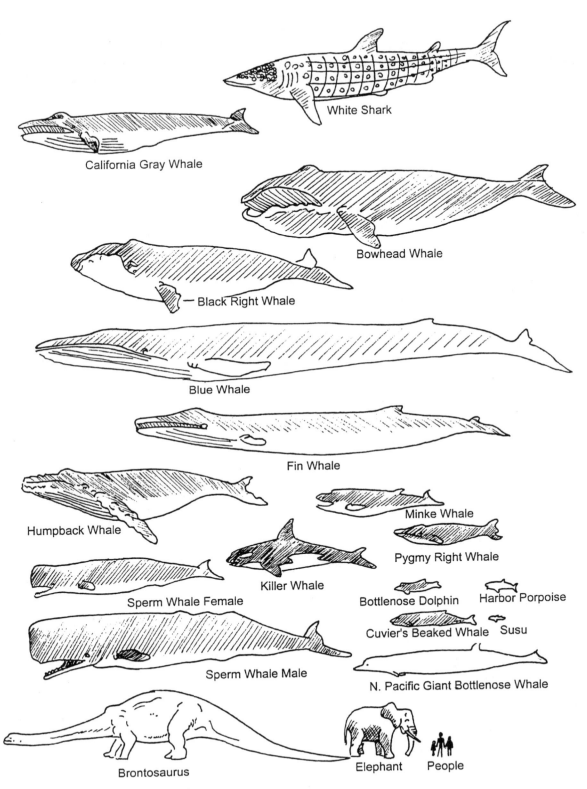

Fig. 2.2. Relative Sizes of Whales.

5. Divide the class into research groups. Ask the library media specialist to help the groups locate materials on whales—e.g., articles about whales in magazines, encyclopedias, books, filmstrips, videos, the Internet, etc. Assign each group a different species of whales to research and have them do a written or oral report. Have groups research the following information about their species of whales:

Anatomy

Feeding habits and food sources

Behaviors (e.g., breaching)

Identifying characteristics

Pathways of migration

Communication

Endangerment

Children should also research general information about the whale as a mammal and information about the whaling industry.

6. Some whales have teeth and eat as people do. Others, including the humpback whale, have a special brushlike structure called baleen. Have children investigate how baleen works (see fig. 2.3). To simulate small marine creatures in the ocean, add pepper to a small bowl filled with water. First, have children use their hands to collect the pepper, then new, clean combs. Which method works better? Why? NOTE: This activity is an adaptation of an experiment by Karen Amodeo available at WhaleNet (http://whale.simmons.edu).

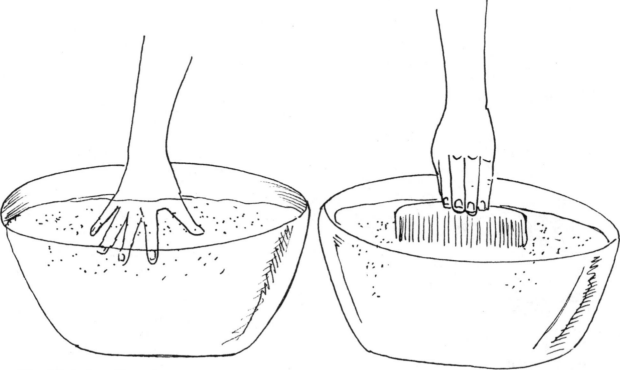

Fig. 2.3. Baleen Experiment.

7. Whales navigate by means of echolocation, an ability similar to the echolocation used by bats. For activities that simulate echolocation, see Chapter 5, "Bats."

8. To bring attention to the plight of the whales and their endangerment, involve children in the creation of "postage stamps." These stamps should include a picture and a conservation-oriented slogan, such as "Save the Whales." The stamps should also include their denomination value.

9. Have children read *Burt Dow, Deep-Water Man* by Robert McCloskey. Discuss the whales that Burt sees and compare them to real whales: Do whales float on top of the water? Are there different colors of whales? What is the meaning of the phrase "Thar' she blows"? How are whales different from fish? How do whales communicate? What is the purpose of a spout?

10. Many "seafaring" words are included in *Burt Dow, Deep-Water Man* by Robert McCloskey. To help children learn these words, use them in context while discussing the book. The words include:

bilge	the lower level of a ship's hold
blubber	whale fat
dory	a small double-ended fishing boat
double-ender	a boat with a pointed bow and stern
gun'l (gunwale)	the upper edge of a boat's side
keel	center piece along the bottom of ship
sediment	matter that settles from a liquid
sou'wester (southwester)	a storm marked by winds from the southwest; a hat worn with raingear
tiller	a bar or handle attached to a boat's rudder

11. Have children listen to whale songs and then attempt imitations with their voices. Have children try imitating songs by making throat noises with their mouth closed. Are there any instruments that might be made to sound like the song of a whale? If a computer with sound capabilities is available, songs of the humpback whale can be heard on the Internet at http://www.gov.nf.ca/itt/business/hmpsound.

12. Many stories of whales have been told over the centuries, from that of Jonah and the whale to tales of Pinocchio and Burt Dow. Have children write a "Whale of a Tale" in which they have an adventure with a whale. The story can be serious or humorous.

13. While listening to the sounds of the humpback whale, have children choreograph a modern-dance interpretation of what they are hearing. Perhaps the physical education teacher can help teach some of the fundamental movements of modern dance.

14. Have the children view the video *Marine Mammals of the Gulf of Maine*, developed by the staff of the College of the Atlantic. This video chronicles the experiences that one might have during a "whale watch." Purchase of the video can be arranged through:

Allied Whale
College of the Atlantic
105 Eden Street
Bar Harbor, ME 04609
(207) 288-5644
www.coa.edu/associated programs
whale@ecology.coa.edu

15. Children might be interested in organizing a fund-raising project to collect donations for "Adopt a Finback Whale," a program managed by the College of the Atlantic in Bar Harbor, Maine (see address under activity 14).

16. The New Bedford Whaling Museum and the Kendall Whaling Museum are potential sources of materials about whales:

New Bedford Whaling Museum
18 Johnny Cake Hill
New Bedford, MA 02740
(509) 997-0046
www.inch.com/~penney/museum/index.htm

The Kendall Whaling Museum
27 Everett Street
Sharon, MA 02067
(617) 784-5642
http://www.kwm.org

17. Word Search—Whaling

    Words or expressions related to whales and the whaling industry are hidden in this word search—horizontally, vertically, and diagonally, forwards and backwards. First, match the "Words Used" to the clues.

CLUES

a. Towards the back of the boat

b. Heavy piece of iron used to hold a boat in place

c. It strains plankton from the seawater

d. Containers for oil

e. Thick layer of fat between the whale's skin and muscle

f. Forward part of the boat

g. Small, flat-bottomed boat

h. Tail of the whale

i. "All hands on _____!"

j. Towards the front of the boat

k. Ship's kitchen

l. Spearlike instrument for fastening onto a whale

m. Warm-blooded animal that nurses its young

n. Large pole for holding rigging and sails

o. Boat being towed through the water by a whale

p. To direct the ship's course

q. Right side of a sailing vessel

r. Left side of a sailing vessel

s. Sailing vessel with two or more masts

t. Officer in charge of a vessel

u. Top of the whale's head

v. Rear end of a vessel

w. It was burned for lighting purposes

x. To measure the depth of water

y. Group or gathering of whales

z. From here came cries of "Land ahoy!"

WORDS USED

aft	deck	navigate
anchor	dory	oil
baleen	flukes	pod
barrels	fore	port
blowhole	galley	schooner
blubber	harpoon	sound
bow	mammal	starboard
captain	mast	stern
crow's nest	Nantucket Sleigh Ride	

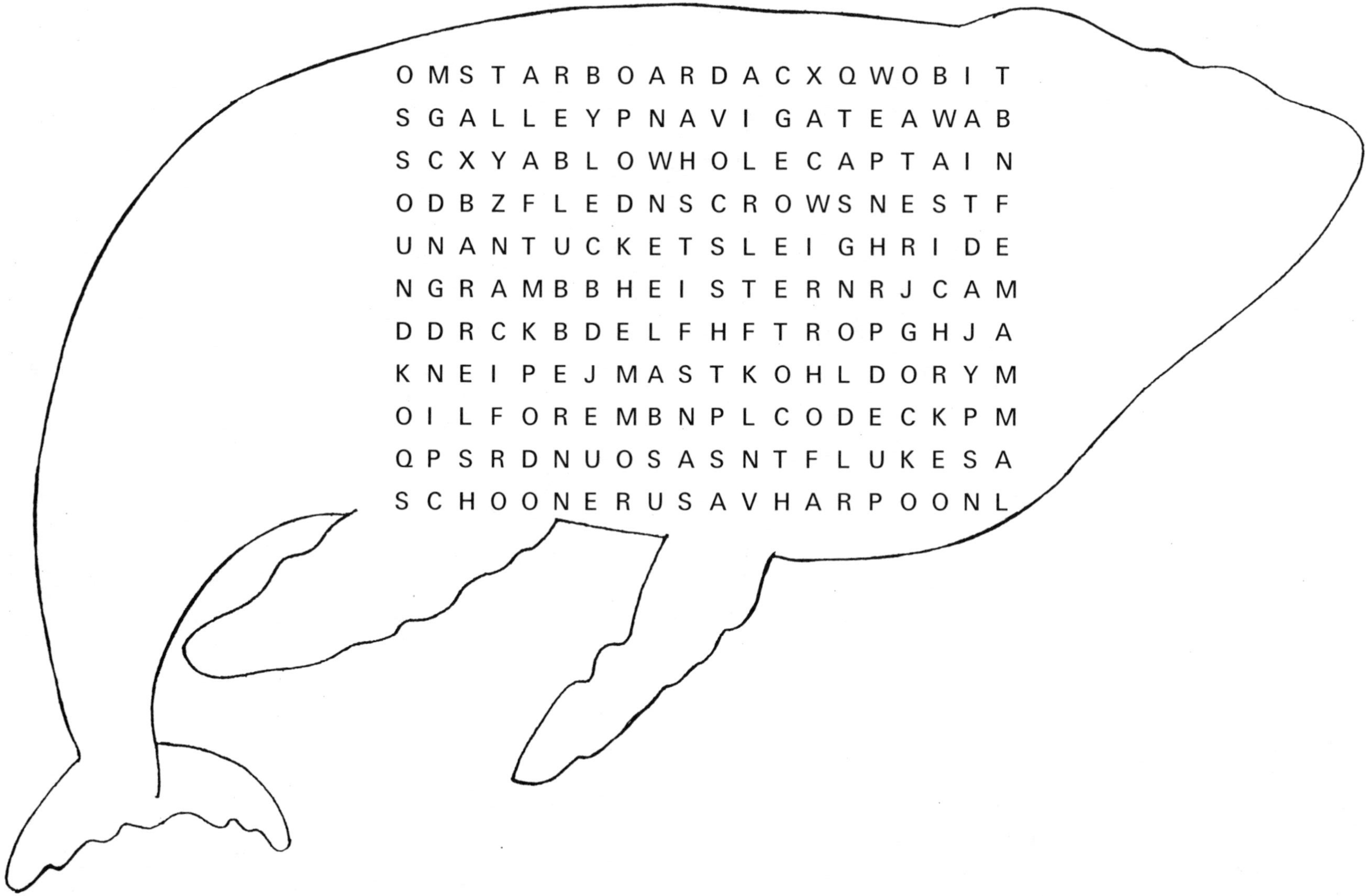

```
O M S T A R B O A R D A C X Q W O B I T
S G A L L E Y P N A V I G A T E A W A B
S C X Y A B L O W H O L E C A P T A I N
O D B Z F L E D N S C R O W S N E S T F
U N A N T U C K E T S L E I G H R I D E
N G R A M B B H E I S T E R N R J C A M
D D R C K B D E L F H F T R O P G H J A
K N E I P E J M A S T K O H L D O R Y M
O I L F O R E M B N P L C O D E C K P M
Q P S R D N U O S A S N T F L U K E S A
S C H O O N E R U S A V H A R P O O N L
```

Fig. 2.4. Word Search—Whaling.

Related Books and References

Jones, Richard. "How Big, How Tall." *Science Scope* 18, no. 11 (October 1995): 22–25.

Katona, Steven, et al. *A Field Guide to the Whales, Porpoises and Seals from Cape Cod to Newfoundland.* Washington, DC: Smithsonian, 1993.

Marine Mammals of the Gulf of Maine. Bar Harbor, ME: Allied Whale, College of the Atlantic. Video.

McCloskey, Robert. *Burt Dow, Deep-Water Man.* New York: Viking, 1963.

Nicklin, Flip. "Bowhead Whales: Leviathans of the Icy Seas." *National Geographic* 188, no. 2 (August 1995): 114–29.

Norris, Kenneth S. "White Whale of the North: Beluga." *National Geographic* 185, no. 6 (June 1994): 2–31.

Payne, Roger. *In the Company of Whales.* New York: Macmillan, 1995.

Sheldon, Dyan. *The Whale's Song.* New York: Dial Books for Young Readers, 1991.

Whitehead, Hal. "The Realm of the Elusive Sperm Whale." *National Geographic* 188, no. 5 (November 1995): 56–73.

Chapter 3

Fish and Aquariums

One Small Fish

by Joanne Ryder
New York: Morrow Junior Books, 1993

Summary

In science class one Friday, all living things are quiet. Even the pump in the fish tank pulses quietly as the waves begin to swell and rise higher and higher. The room sinks like a ship in the sea as a young girl in the classroom is transported beneath the waves. From there, she sees octopi, eels, porpoises, and a school of fish, all of which disappear when class is over—except for one small fish, which follows the girl home.

Science and Content Related Concepts

Aquarium management, saltwater fish, freshwater fish

Content Related Words

Aquarium, tank, moss, octopus, starfish, eel, seal, dolphin, shark, fish

Activities

1. Set up a freshwater aquarium for the classroom (see fig. 3.1). You will need the following items:

10-gallon aquarium tank	Filter charcoal
Air pump	Air tubing
Aquarium heater	10 pounds aquarium gravel
Aquarium filter	Aquarium thermometer
Filter floss	Aquarium cover (optional)

   a. Locate the aquarium near an electric outlet (for the heater and the pump) on a level place that is out of the way of classroom traffic. Do not place it near a radiator. The aquarium needs to be set up and the filter and pump should be run for several days before the fish are introduced.

b. First, wash the aquarium carefully with clear water. Never wash the aquarium with soap or chemicals. Rinse the gravel several times with clear water to eliminate fine particles that can clog the fish's gills and choke them. Place the washed gravel into the aquarium and fill the aquarium with cold tap water. (Before adding the water, place an old saucer or a small plate on top of the gravel to keep the water from disturbing it.) Fill the aquarium until the water level is about two inches below the top. Attach the filter and air pump. Finally, attach the heater and thermometer and remove the saucer.

c. To remove impurities from the water, and to ensure that the water will be well aerated, cover the aquarium and run the filter and pump for several days before introducing the fish. The ideal temperature for the water is 70 to 80 degrees Fahrenheit. If plants are desired for the aquarium, it is best to add them at this time. Pet store personnel can suggest a selection of plants well suited for particular aquarium setups.

d. An aquarium should not be crowded with fish. A recommended starting population is one catfish (or "algae eater"), three neons, four guppies, and five snails. Fish are usually sold in water-filled plastic bags. Before introducing the fish into the aquarium, float the bags on the water in the aquarium to equalize the temperature. Then, carefully puncture the bags and release the fish and water into the aquarium. After the fish have been in the aquarium for about half an hour, give them a little food. Feed the fish each day, but be careful not to overfeed them. Establish and observe a regular feeding schedule. Provide a larger feeding before weekends or holidays, or use time released food tablets. NOTE: From time to time, add small quantities of water to replace evaporated water. It is preferable to allow the water to set overnight before adding it to the aquarium.

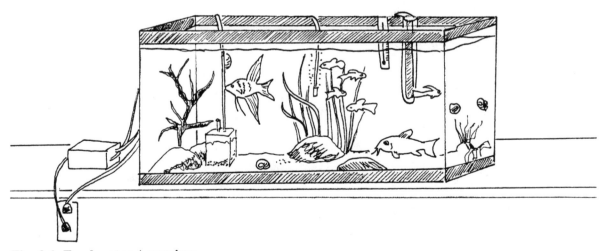

Fig. 3.1. Freshwater Aquarium.

2. Set up a station in the classroom where a "Fish Log" can be maintained. Each day, assign a pair of children to feed the fish and to observe the conditions in the aquarium: How many fish are there? Is the water clear or cloudy? Does it appear that the previous day's feeding was consumed? Is it necessary to give the fish additional food? What is the temperature of the water? Do any fish appear ill or sluggish? Make a log chart in which the children who are feeding the fish can reply to the questions asked in the log.

3. Have children learn to spell the following words, which they will need to use when recording information in the "Fish Log" (see activity 2). These words will also be used in the "Freshwater Aquarium" crossword puzzle (see activity 15).

angel fish	gravel	pump
aquarium	guppy	snail
catfish (algae eater)	neon	water
filter	plant	

4. Hand out a list of various story starters related to setting up an aquarium. Allow children free time to write their stories. Add story starters to the following list, as desired.

   If I were one of the plants (or animals) in the aquarium . . .

   The strange people on the other side of the glass . . .

   When I first came to my new home in your classroom . . .

   Getting used to my new home . . .

   I was swimming along in the water when . . .

   It's a lot of fun being a fish because . . .

5. Have children make a shoe box aquarium by drawing an underwater scene on the inside bottom of a shoe box. Have them draw, color, and cut out various fish shapes to hang with string or yarn inside the box, creating a three-dimensional effect (see fig. 3.2). To create a large-scale diorama, have children draw an underwater scene on the chalkboard or bulletin board. Hang large plants and cutouts of water creatures from the ceiling.

Fig. 3.2. Shoe Box Aquarium.

6. Have children each make a large drawing of a fish (see fig. 3.3), using large sheets of construction paper, newsprint, or butcher paper. The fish should be about 24 inches long. Once the drawing has been made, have children cut out the original and one copy. Staple or stitch together (using an overcast darning stitch) the edges of the two fish cutouts, leaving the mouth area open. Crumple half sheets of newspaper and stuff the fish until it puffs out and becomes three-dimensional. Finally, tie a string onto the mouth. Have children "fly" their fish by waving them on the playground. NOTE: Reinforce the area where the string attaches to the fish to prevent ripping. Pieces of cellophane tape work well.

7. Have children make textured fish. Draw an outline of a large fish on a piece of cardboard and cut out the fish. Color macaroni pieces as desired to decorate the fish. (To color macaroni, mix 1 tablespoon food coloring with a half cup of water in a small mixing bowl. Add 1 cup dry elbow macaroni to the liquid and "toss" gently. Lay colored macaroni on absorbent towels for several hours. It is not recommended to soak the macaroni as the shells will split.) Glue the macaroni onto the cardboard fish in stripes, waves, and other "fishy" designs. Children may want to invent camouflage coloration that make the fish more visible or more invisible.

8. Have children compare their fish masterpieces with the fish in Leo Lionni's *Fish Is Fish*. What are the similarities and differences? What is the meaning of the title of this book.

9. If you live near the sea, you might want to set up a saltwater aquarium (see fig. 3.4) for the classroom:

   a. The saltwater aquarium can be set up in the same manner as the freshwater aquarium (see activity 1), except that a heater is not required and sand or gravel from the seashore should be substituted for the aquarium gravel. (NOTE: A thermometer is still essential to the set-up of the saltwater aquarium.) Collect enough seawater to fill the aquarium. It is best to collect sea creatures from the same location as the water. Place the aquarium in the coolest part of the room.

   b. Sea creatures for a saltwater aquarium might include a few examples of each of the following:

      Clams

      Crabs

      Mussels

      Sand dollars

      Sea cucumbers

      Small intertidal-zone fish

      Snails

      Starfish

   Be sure to provide more clams and mussels than any other creature as they will be eaten by the starfish and crabs.

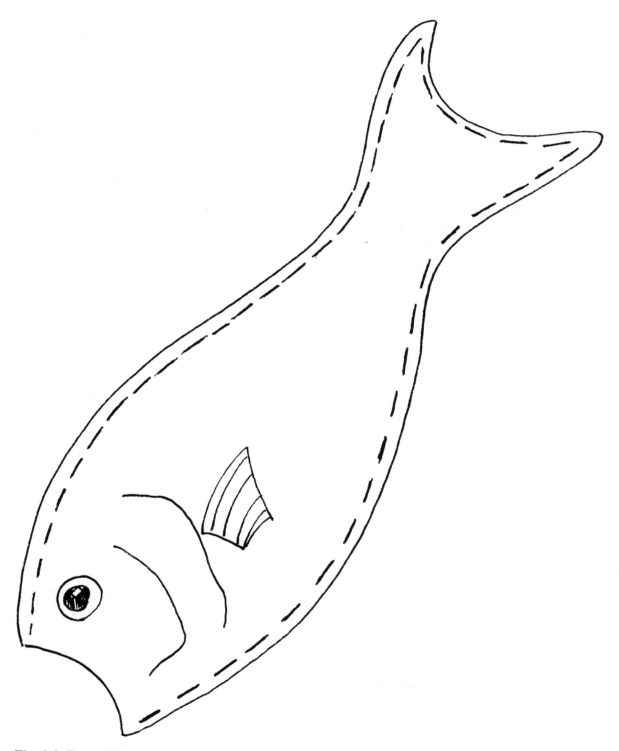

Fig. 3.3. Paper Fish.

c. It is not necessary to feed a saltwater aquarium. If properly set up, it will be self-perpetuating. The creatures and the algae that grow in the water will provide food for each other.

d. The temperature of the water should be kept at about room temperature (68°F). There are two methods for cooling the water: 1) put ice into tightly sealed bags and float them on the surface of the sea water, but do not allow the fresh water to enter the salt water, and; 2) keep bottles of sea water refrigerated and add them to the aquarium, after removing the same amount of warmer water. Put the warm water into the refrigerator for cooling. Repeat the process as needed. If the temperature is 68°F or cooler, this step is unnecessary.

e. Water will continually evaporate from the aquarium. Draw a line at the top of the tank when it is full; maintain the water level at this line by replacing evaporated water with small amounts of tap water. Let the water sit in an open container for a day before adding it to the tank (this allows chlorine to dissipate).

f. Have children learn to spell the names of the sea creatures in the aquarium, as well as the parts of the aquarium. Have them keep a daily observation log of the aquarium, as explained in activity 2. The major difference will be that the sea creatures will eat each another. Replace these creatures as needed.

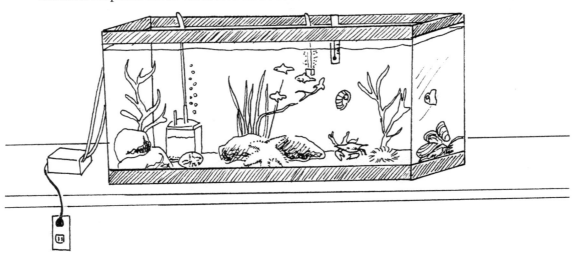

Fig. 3.4. Saltwater Aquarium.

10. Sea creatures live and act quite differently than freshwater creatures. Have children study the sea creatures in the saltwater aquarium and create a pantomime that shows how they move, eat, and digest food.

11. "Fold-a-puppets" are a fun way to introduce dramatic activities related to the sea creatures in the saltwater aquarium. Fold an 8½-by-11-inch sheet of paper, as shown in figure 3.5a. Paste a picture of a sea creature (see figs. 3.5b and 3.5c) onto the puppet. Have children present brief puppet skits, answering these questions:

How do I live?

What body parts do I have?

How do I move?

How do I eat?

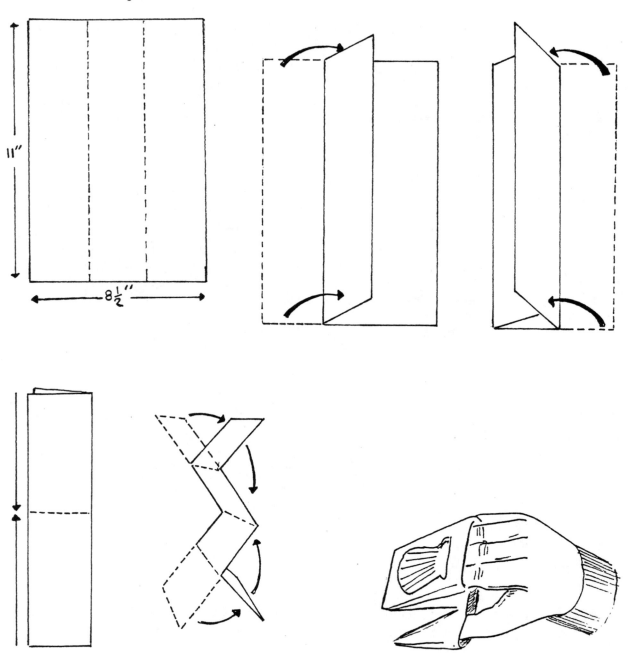

Fig. 3.5a. Fold-a-Puppets.

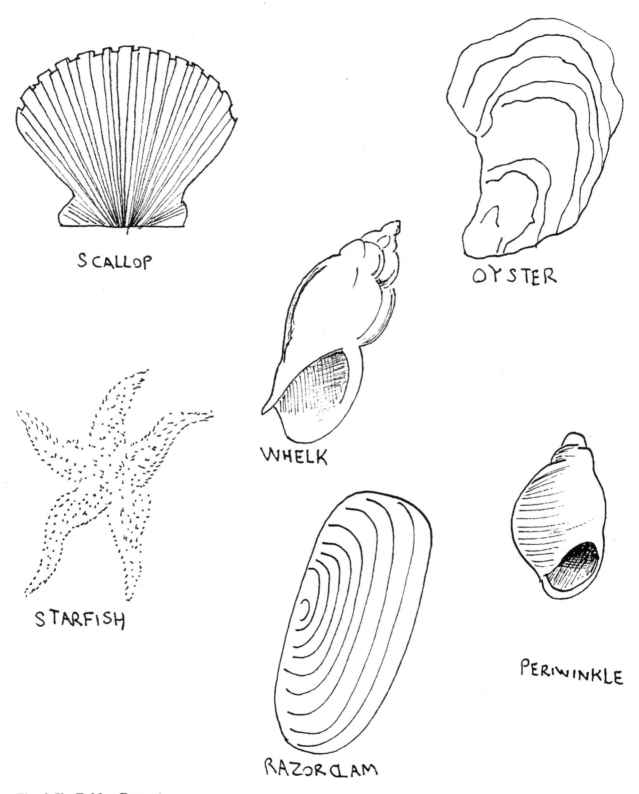

SCALLOP

OYSTER

WHELK

STARFISH

RAZOR CLAM

PERIWINKLE

Fig. 3.5b. Fold-a-Puppets.

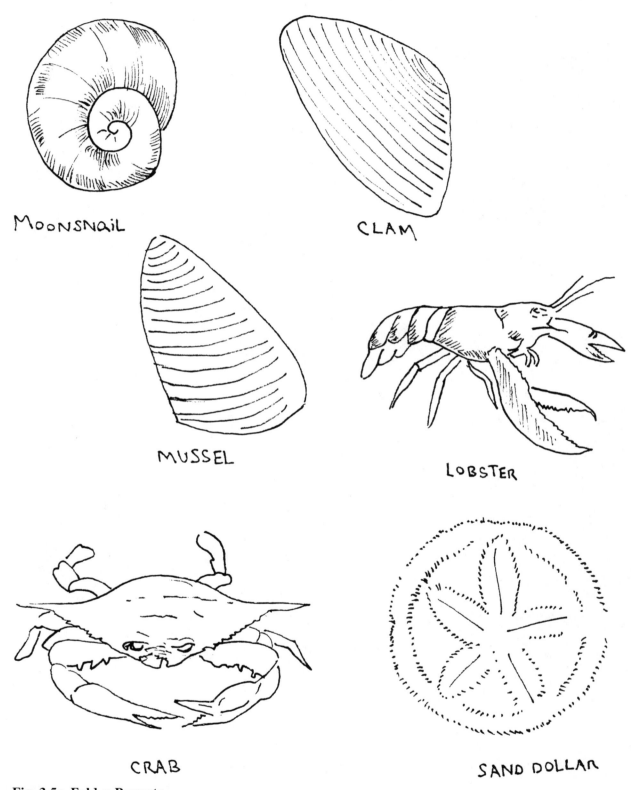

Fig. 3.5c. Fold-a-Puppets.

12. Visit the fish section of a local grocery store or fish distributor to observe the many species of saltwater fish and other sea creatures. How are they different from freshwater creatures? Back in the classroom, have children make a book of pictures illustrating their visit. For very young children, have them dictate a brief story to the teacher, who writes it on the child's paper. If conditions are favorable, you may wish to sample a variety of the items from the sea. Ask adults to help you organize a "Taste of the Sea" snack time in which the class samples several varieties of seafood.

13. Visit a local aquarium, pet store, or grocery store where tanks of live sea creatures are maintained. For each fish or sea creature observed, ask children to describe how it moves. How is it shaped? What helps to keep its body shape? What body parts does it have? Does it make sounds? As children observe the sea creatures, have them make sketches that will later develop into more elaborate drawings in the classroom. Collect the drawings to make a classroom display, or make copies of a few drawings to include in a newsletter sent home to parents.

14. If only these creatures could talk! Have children pretend to be one of the freshwater or saltwater creatures in the aquariums. They could tell a tale of the adventure they had when they were moved from their native home to the classroom.

15. Crossword—Freshwater Aquarium

CLUES

Across

1. Fish with a large tail

4. Where fish live in the classroom

5. Fish with a bright line down its side

9. Fish that lives on the bottom of the aquarium

10. Creature that creeps along the side of the aquarium

Down

2. Something green that grows in the aquarium

3. It pushes air into the aquarium

4. Fish with stripes down its body (two words)

6. Fish swim and thrive in this liquid

7. Rocks at the bottom of the aquarium

8. Removes impurities from the water

WORDS USED

angel fish
aquarium
catfish
filter

gravel
guppy
neon
plant

pump
snail
water

Fig. 3.6. Crossword—Freshwater Aquarium.

16. Crossword—Saltwater Aquarium

CLUES

Across

4. It sounds more like a vegetable (two words)

7. You can't "spend" this creature (two words)

8. Small inhabitants of the intertidal zone

Down

1. Critter with two shells that hangs onto rocks with a beardlike substance

2. Its "heavenly" shape is made up of five arms

3. Animal with 10 appendages that walks sideways

5. "Slow as a _____."

6. Animal that moves by means of a large foot, which comes out from between its two shells

WORDS USED

clam	mussel	snail
crab	sand dollar	starfish
fish	sea cucumber	

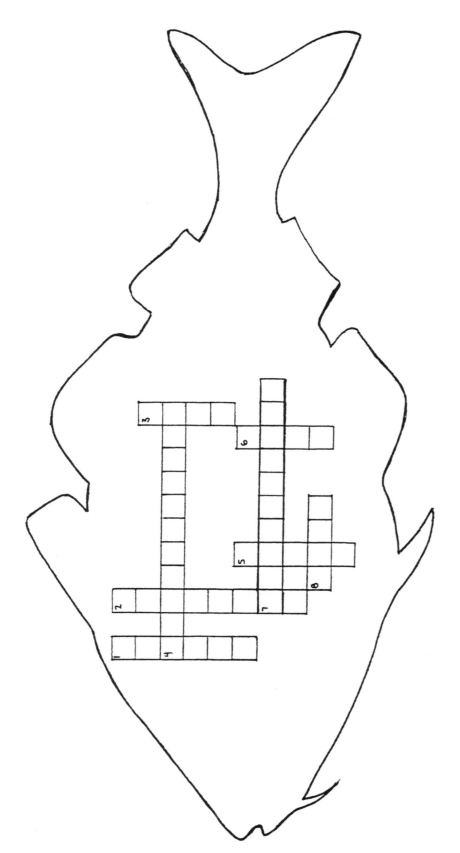

Fig. 3.7. Crossword—Saltwater Aquarium.

Related Books and References

Halstead, Bruce W., and Bonnie L. Landa. *Tropical Fish.* New York: Golden Press, 1975.

Lionni, Leo. *Fish Is Fish*. New York: Pantheon Books, 1970.

Chapter 4

Life at the Shore

One Morning in Maine

by Robert McCloskey
New York: Viking, 1952

Summary

When Sal finds she has a loose tooth, she shares her joy with her family and the animals near her home. Unfortunately, when the tooth comes out, Sal loses it on the beach, and she then fears that her wish will not be fulfilled. However, many pleasant surprises come to her that day.

Science and Content Related Concepts

Change, aging, growing up, dental hygiene, marine life, food chain, predator-prey relationships

Content Related Words

Tooth, sea gull, fish hawk, loon, seal, herring, feather, clam, mussel, outboard motor

Activities

1. On a map of the United States (see fig. 4.1), have children locate Maine. Notice the relationship of this state to the Atlantic Ocean. From the words and pictures in the story, where might Sal and Jane have lived? How would children describe their home and community?

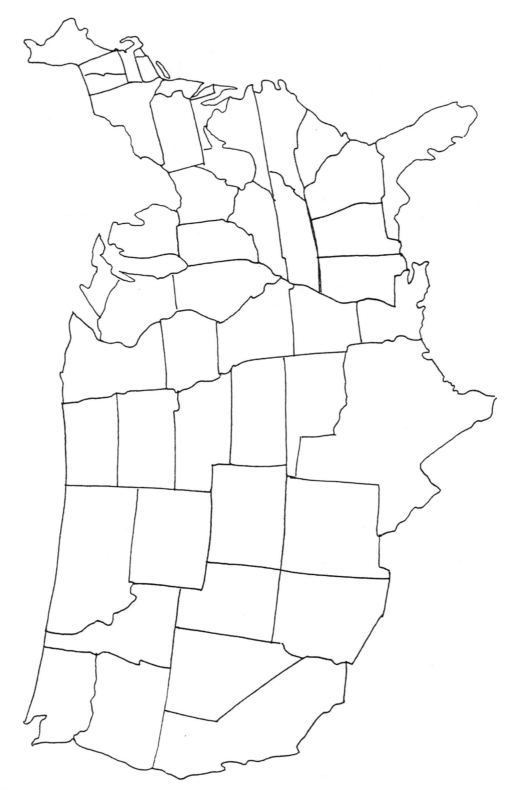

Fig. 4.1. Map of the United States.

From *More Science Through Children's Literature*. © 1998 Butzow and Butzow. Teacher Ideas Press. (800) 237-6124.

2. Aquaculture is an exciting new method of reproducing all varieties of sea animals. Have children practice their Internet skills by searching the Web using the word *aquaculture*. What is aquaculture? What varieties of sea life are grown in these controlled circumstances? Where are aquaculture sites located? What other countries are involved in aquaculture? Where can names and addresses of persons who are involved in this venture be obtained? Have children share and discuss the information they find at this Web site.

3. Clams and mussels are edible and can be made into a thick soup called chowder. Have children try this recipe:

> 2 onions, diced
> 4 potatoes, diced
> 4 cups milk
> 4 tablespoons margarine
> 1 teaspoon salt
> $\frac{1}{2}$ teaspoon pepper
> 1 can (14$\frac{1}{2}$ ounces) creamed corn (optional)
> 1 6$\frac{1}{2}$-ounce can minced clams/mussels OR
> > 1 cup fresh clams/mussels

In a heavy kettle, combine all ingredients and simmer for 1 to 1$\frac{1}{2}$ hours, stirring often. NOTE: Fresh clams and mussels are usually available at the seafood counter of grocery stores. Let children feel and examine the shells before you cook them. To steam open clams or mussels, place them in a large pot filled with about two inches of water. Cover, bring to a boil, then simmer for about five minutes, or until the shells open. Let cool before handling. Discard any shells that did not open while being steamed.

After steaming open the clam or mussel shells, have children remove the meat. Have them observe the interior and exterior of the shell. Point out the growth rings on the exterior and the muscle scars inside (see fig. 4.2). Steaming can be done in a deep fryer or electric skillet, if a kitchen is not available.

Interior of Shell

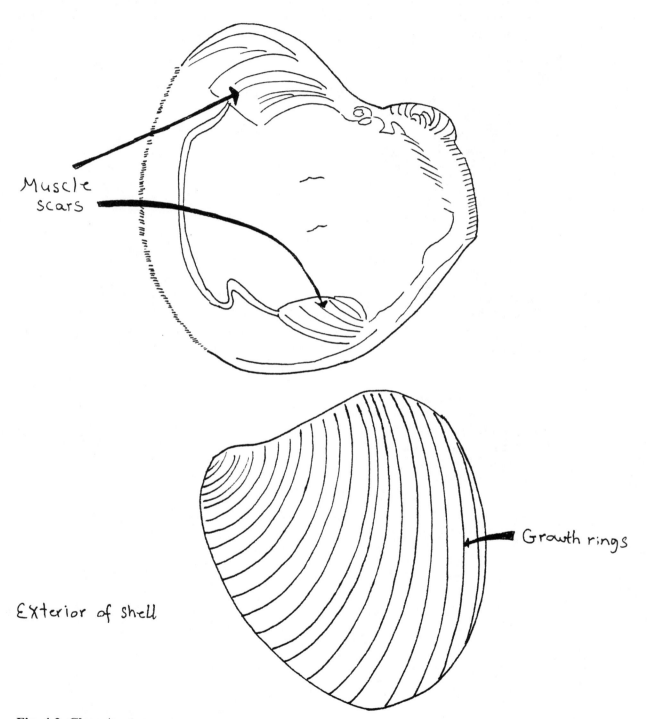

Muscle
scars

Growth rings

Exterior of Shell

Fig. 4.2. Clam Anatomy.

4. For a dessert to follow the chowder, have children make ice cream!

Vanilla Ice Cream

1½ cups whole milk
¾ cup sugar
dash salt
1 tablespoon vanilla
2 egg yolks
1 cup whipping cream
1 cup cream

Scald milk. Add sugar and salt; stir until dissolved. Beat egg yolks separately, then stir slowly into milk mixture. Cook until thick, stirring constantly at moderate heat. Add remaining ingredients; mix. Let the mixture cool for two to three hours. Churn in an ice cream freezer as directed in the instructions for the freezer.

Chocolate Ice Cream

To make chocolate ice cream, follow the above recipe, but increase whole milk to 2 cups, increase sugar to 1 cup, and add 2 ounces melted baking chocolate.

5. Take a survey of children's favorite flavors of ice cream. Have children make a bar graph to show favorite flavors for the entire class (see fig. 4.3).

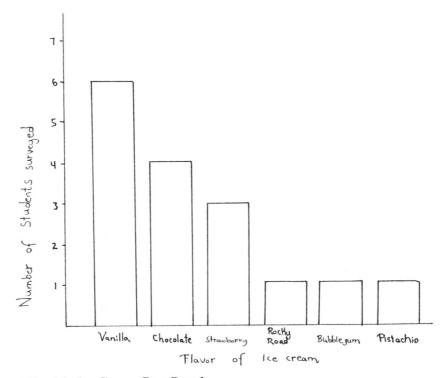

Fig. 4.3. Ice Cream Bar Graph.

6. *One Morning in Maine* is a story of the changes taking place in Sal and Jane's life. Their life is very different from modern life in the United States, yet there are many similarities. Have children compare Sal and Jane's life to theirs, using words and pictures as evidence to support their claims.

7. After children have compared their life to Sal and Jane's life, have them imagine themselves as babies, youngsters, teenagers, and adults. Have children make drawings of these four periods in their life.

8. Knowing the various Maine birds was an important part of Sal's life. Ask children what birds are common to their area. Do these birds migrate in the fall? Are the birds protected by any agencies? Invite a bird lover or ornithologist to visit the class and discuss these topics and answer any questions children have.

9. Have children erect a bird feeder in a place where birds can be observed. Have them keep track of the kinds of birds that come to the feeder, noting approximately how many of each kind visit. Make bar graphs to show which kinds are most common (see fig. 4.4). Which ones are rare? Do particular kinds only come at particular times of the day or year? What scares them away? NOTE: If children erect a bird feeder, the birds will become dependent on them for food. Do not set up a feeder unless children (or you) can continue to provide food.

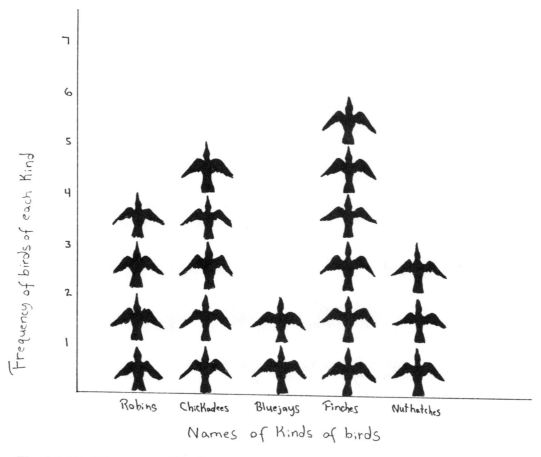

Fig. 4.4. Bird Frequency Graph.

10. Have children examine a bird feather using a magnifying lens. Look for the quill, the shaft, the barbs, and the barbules (see fig. 4.5). How does this construction help protect birds from the elements? How do feathers help the bird shed water? How do the feathers help them fly? NOTE: Feathers can be obtained from a mail order company that sells materials for making fishing flies or from discarded pillows or down clothing. Feathers found on the ground are not sanitary and should not be touched by children.

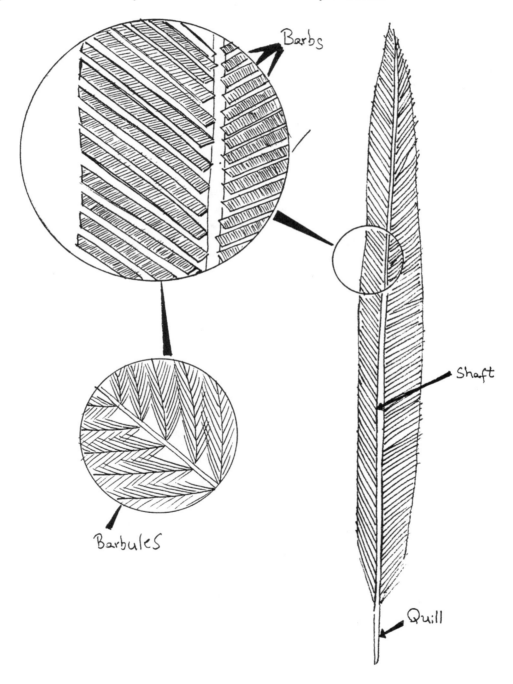

Fig. 4.5. Feather.

11. A discussion of dental hygiene might naturally follow a reading of *One Morning in Maine*. Discuss with children how many teeth a human being has and the purposes of the various teeth. Study the parts of a tooth (see fig. 4.6). Ask a dentist or dental hygienist to visit the class and discuss proper toothcare, including brushing, flossing, eating healthy foods, and orthodontia.

12. Using a large paper cutout of a tooth, have children write on it the secret wish they would have if they were in Sal's place. Ask children if their wish could be fulfilled.

13. The performance of small internal combustion engines, such as the outboard motor in *One Morning in Maine*, can be fascinating. Invite someone who repairs engines to visit the class and demonstrate the parts of an engine and how it works. Have children ask questions, such as: What are the most important parts of the engine? What is the role of the spark plug? What maintenance is necessary for a small engine?

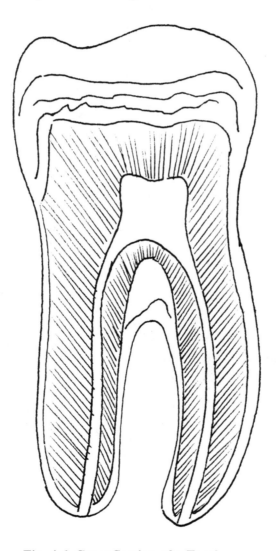

Fig. 4.6. Cross Section of a Tooth.

14. Have children search the Internet using the term *outboard motor*. Have them compare the motors they read about or see there to the motor that Mr. Condon repaired in the story. What else can children learn from the Internet about these small engines ?

15. Spark plugs are essential to the operation of a small engine. Using figure 4.7 as an example, have children write and illustrate an advertisement to promote their own special brand of spark plugs.

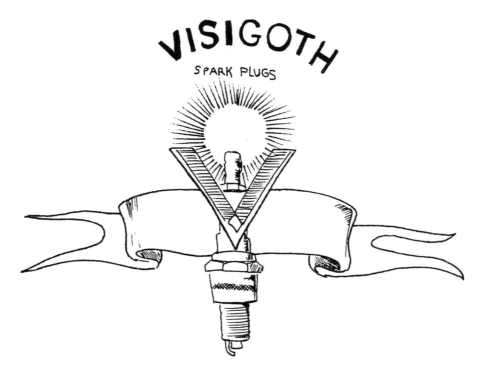

Fig. 4.7. Advertisement for Spark Plugs.

16. Have children try art projects using clam, mussel, or other seashells. Soak the shells in diluted chlorine bleach and clean them thoroughly with an old toothbrush. Let the shells dry before using them. NOTE: Mussels can be obtained at the grocery. Use the insides for chowder, then recycle the shells. They are also very common on sea shores and even some lakes.

Shell Animals

Materials

Shells, cloth pieces, paper scraps, craft eyes, white glue, scissors, markers, other decorative materials

Procedure

Design and cut out paper and cloth body parts for animals. Glue designs of decorative materials onto the shells.

Challenge

Make a pet shell.

Wood/Shell Sculpture

Materials

Shells, pieces of driftwood or small pieces of wood, white glue, sandpaper

Procedure

Glue shells in a pattern onto a piece of wood.

Challenge

Sand a piece of wood so that it can be set squarely on a table or shelf as a decoration.

Shell Chimes

Materials

Shells, coat hanger or tree branch, strong thread or yarn, electric drill

Procedure

Drill a hole in the end of each shell (an adult should do this). Attach the shells to a coat hanger or tree branch using strong thread or yarn (see fig. 4.8).

Challenge

Construct the chimes so that they "ring" when blowing in a breeze.

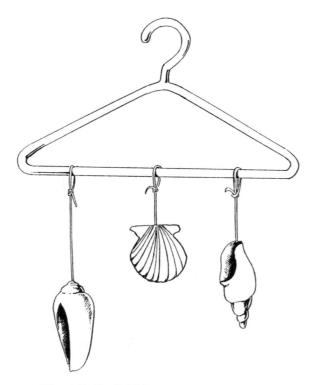

Fig. 4.8. Shell Chimes.

17. Word Ladder—Seaweed

Seaweed is a common sight on the coast of Maine. Solve the clues for this word ladder using an encyclopedia for help. Write the answers in the puzzle blanks, which are formed around the words *Sargasso Sea*—a vast area in the Atlantic Ocean with a high concentration of seaweed.

CLUES

1. I attach myself to _____ so that I can stay in one spot.

2. I am a small, bubblelike part of seaweed that enables it to _____ in the water.

3. I am a green pigment in plants. I am called _____ .

4. I am a common color for seaweed. I am _____ .

5. I am a member of a large group of water plants known as _____ .

6. I am a tough leathery seaweed called _____ _____ . I am important as a source of agar.

7. I am a plant that lives in ocean waters. I can be green, red, or brown. I am _____ .

8. I am given off by seaweed and help keep the water pure. I am _____ .

9. I am the great brown algae of northern waters known as _____ .

10. I am rich in potash, so I can be used in the manufacture of _____ .

11. I am a thickening agent used in the preparation of soup. I am _____ .

WORDS USED

agar	float	oxygen
algae	green	rocks
chlorophyll	Irish moss	seaweed
fertilizer	kelps	

From *More Science Through Children's Literature*. © 1998 Butzow and Butzow. Teacher Ideas Press. (800) 237-6124.

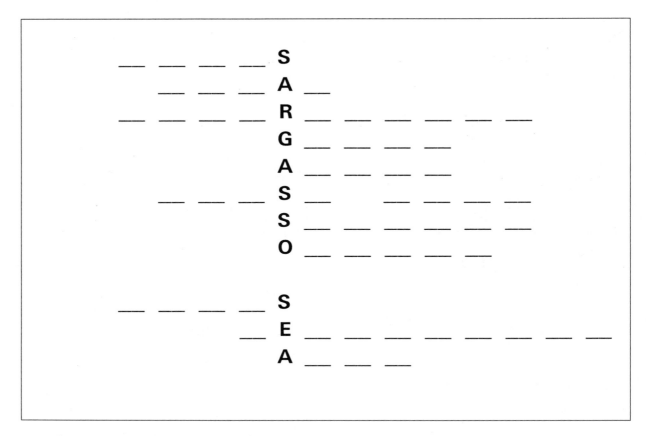

Fig. 4.9. Word Ladder—Seaweed.

Related Books and References

Cole, Joanna. *The Magic School Bus on the Ocean Floor*. New York: Scholastic, 1992.

McCloskey, Robert. *Blueberries for Sal*. New York: Viking, 1948.

———. *Burt Dow, Deep-Water Man*. New York: Viking, 1963.

Let's Explore a Seashore. Washington, DC: National Geographic Society. 15 min. Videocassette number 51607.

Sterling, Donna R. "Why Feathers and Oil Don't Mix." *Science Scope* 18, no. 4 (January 1995): 32–35.

Zim, Herbert S., and Lester Ingle. *Seashores*. New York: Simon & Schuster, 1955.

Chapter 5

Bats

Stellaluna

by Janell Cannon
San Diego, CA: Harcourt Brace Jovanovich, 1993

Summary

When Stellaluna was knocked from her mother's grasp by the owl, she ended up in a nest with three small birds. To adapt to her new surroundings, Stellaluna learned to eat bugs without making a face and to sleep in the nest rather than hang upside down by her feet. Then, the day she went for flying lessons with the birds, she found her mother, who promised Stellaluna that she would never have to eat another bug. NOTE: Stellaluna was a fruit bat and did not eat bugs; many species of bats do eat bugs, however.

Science and Content Related Concepts

Predator-prey relationships, mother-child relationships, survival techniques, animal instincts, friendship

Content Related Words

Mammal, endangered species, dispersal, guano, nocturnal, pollination, ecosystem

Activities

1. Several weeks before beginning this unit, contact the Bat Conservation International (BCI) at 1-800-538-2287, or visit their Web site at http://www.batcon.org. BCI will send fact sheets about bats, teaching ideas, and a gift catalog, along with information on becoming a member of BCI. Other information can be found by browsing the Web site.

2. Also before reading *Stellaluna*, to understand better the prejudices and misconceptions that people often have about bats, ask parents, other adults, and children in the class what they believe about bats. Write down these comments and compile the results. Arrange the statements under two headings—"Positive Comments" (e.g., bats eat insects) and "Negative Comments" (e.g., bats suck blood). Which group of statements is longer? How can children learn the truth about bats and overcome many of these negative misconceptions?

49

3. Explain to children the usage of phrases, such as "Blind as a bat," "Bats in the belfry," and "Gone batty." Which phrases would be considered positive? Negative?

4. The name *Stellaluna* is made up of two Latin words—*stella* and *luna*. Have children look up these words to learn the meaning of the name *Stellaluna*.

5. Echolocation is a sounding device that enables bats to "see" in the dark. Essentially, the bat uses its ears as eyes. It emits a high-frequency sound, which bounces back to it from objects. This process gives the bat an indication of the objects in front of it. Have children work in pairs to simulate this process: Hold a sheet of paper in front of your face and making a repetitive sound, such as "hoo-hoo-hoo," while bringing the paper closer to your lips (see fig. 5.1). Have the child who is listening wear a blindfold to lessen distractions. Listen to how the sound changes as the paper comes closer to the lips. Does it make a difference if the paper is folded in half or at an angle? Do different kinds of papers echo sounds differently? What happens if a jar, oatmeal box, or other container is used? Give each child a chance to be the listener.

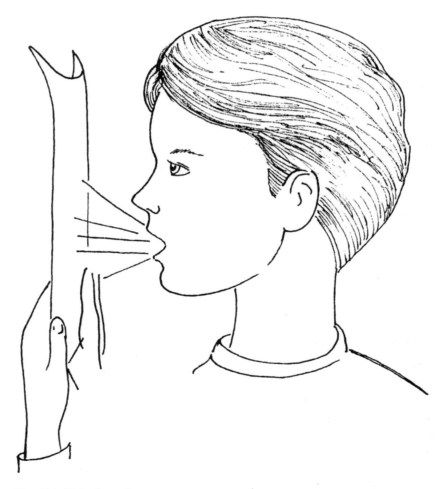

Fig. 5.1. Echolocation.

6. Have children try this activity to simulate echolocation: Choose one child, who is blind-folded, to play the role of the bat. The other children stand still around the room, representing rocks, trees, animals, and so on. The child who is the bat tries to walk across the room without bumping into any of the children. This child says "bat, bat, bat" while moving across the room. The objects also say "bat, bat, bat" as the child comes near them. Using these auditory clues, the child who is the bat can avoid bumping into anything by using only their sense of hearing. NOTE: Push desks, chairs, and other objects out of the way and give children plenty of space to maneuver.

7. Some people think that bats are birds, but in reality, they are mammals. Make a class chart with "Bats" and "Birds" as headings. In the library media center, have children research bats and birds. After they have learned how bats and birds are similar and different, have children fill in the chart. NOTE: Many insects also move about by flying. If desired, add a third column, "Insects," to the chart, and have children compare how insects are similar to and different from bats and birds.

8. Have children research various species of bats and make trivia cards that might be placed on the bulletin board or in another area of the classroom. Trivia might include facts, such as:

   Indonesian flying foxes have wing spans of up to six feet in length.

   A three-inch brown bat with a wing span of 10 inches can catch 600 mosquitoes in one hour.

9. Using the library media center and the Internet, have children research what they would like to know about bats (e.g., sizes, physical descriptions, where they live, what they eat, their uses to humanity, how they protect themselves, whether or not they use echolocation, etc.). Remind children that there are about 1,000 species of bats, ranging from the brown bat, which could fit in the palm of a hand, to the Indonesian flying fox, which can have a wingspan of up to six feet in length. NOTE: BCI's Web site (http://www.batcon.org) is a good resource for this activity.

10. Using all that they have learned, have each child make a fact card about their favorite kind of bat, then make a drawing or mask of this bat for a bulletin board display. Ask children what they have learned about bats that is different than what they thought at the beginning of the unit. What important facts about bats would children tell people now?

11. Have children access information about bats on the Internet at http://sln.fi.edu/inquirer/bats.html, a site compiled by the *Philadelphia Inquirer.*

12. Bats often live in abandoned mines, yet in many areas these mines are being sealed as a safety precaution. When a mine is sealed, the bats die because they cannot leave the mine to find food. Have children work in groups to produce and videotape a class "infomercial" about the necessity of preserving bat habitats. They should stress the positive nature of bats and why abandoned mines should be allowed to continue to provide a home for the bats. Have groups produce a television commercial, a radio public service announcement, and a newspaper feature article. NOTE: To seal a mine, a large gate can be constructed over the mine opening so that curious persons will be kept out, but the bats will continue to have free access to the mine.

13. Have a "Bat Appreciation Day" for children to share the many things they have learned about bats and the projects they have completed (e.g., trivia cards, comparison chart of bats and birds). Celebrate with a cake made in the shape of a bat (see fig. 5.2).

Fig. 5.2. Bat Cake.

14. Bats are excellent fliers because of the way their wings have evolved. Have children use their creative skills to invent a paper airplane with wings similar to the wings of a bat (see fig. 5.3). Have contests to see which airplanes go the farthest and the highest. Which design is the best performer for flying? NOTE: Refer to Chapter 20, "Kites, Wind, and Flight," and Chapter 21, "Airplanes and Flight," for more information about flight.

Fig. 5.3. Bat Wings.

15. Have children dramatize the story of *Stellaluna*. They may write a script based on the story in the book or pantomime the action. Have children act out further adventures that Stellaluna might have, alone or with her friends.

16. Often in folklore, bats are considered to be evil creatures that live with witches or Count Dracula. Have children "rewrite" history by writing stories in which bats are "the good guys" and do much to help humans.

17. Word Ladder—Bats

     Using all that you have learned about bats, fill in the answers to this word ladder, which are formed around the words *endangered species*. First, match the words to the clues.

CLUES

1. Sensing device that helps locate prey

2. To take pollen from one plant to another

3. Animal that preys on another animal

4. Desert plant pollinated by bats

5. Having to do with nighttime

6. Bat droppings

7. Ecological community

8. Dense, tropical forest (two words)

9. Science of raising crops

10. To break up and scatter

11. Warm-blooded animals

12. Mistaken or wrong idea

13. Species of bats that suck blood (two words)

14. Bugs that bats eat

15. Natural environment where an animal lives

16. To sleep through the winter

17. Species of bats known by their color (two words)

WORDS USED

agriculture	habitat	pollination
cactus	hibernation	predator
disperse	insects	rain forest
echolocation	mammals	red bats
ecosystem	misconception	vampire bats
guano	nocturnal	

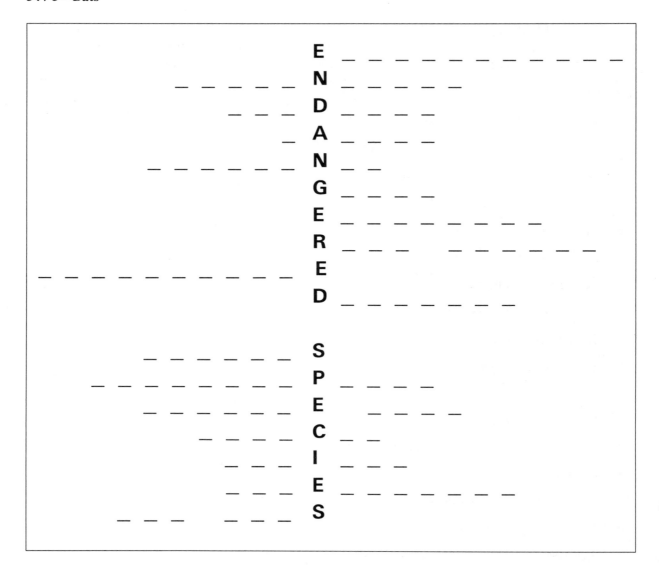

Fig. 5.4. Word Ladder—Bats.

Related Books and References

McKee, Judith. "Bat Facts and Fun." *Science and Children* 30, no. 2 (October 1992): 26–29.

Mollel, Tololwa. *A Promise to the Sun: An African Story.* Boston: Joy Street Books, 1992.

Strauss, Johann, Jr. *Die Fledermaus.* Vienna State Opera Orchestra. Herbert von Karajan.

Tuttle, Merlin D. "Saving North America's Beleaguered Bats." *National Geographic* 188, no. 2 (August 1995): 37–57.

Chapter 6

Life Cycle of Trees

Red Leaf, Yellow Leaf

by Lois Ehlert
San Diego, CA: Harcourt Brace Jovanovich, 1991

Summary

From a tiny seed to a strong, young sapling, the life of a sugar maple tree is described by the young boy who picked out the tree and planted it.

Science and Content Related Concepts

Life cycle of the tree, seasons of the year, parts of the tree, characteristics of the tree, selecting and planting trees, seed dispersal and growth

Content Related Words

Winged seeds, roots, sprouts, transplant, habitat, nursery. NOTE: This story should be read three times during the school year—in fall, in winter, and in spring. By doing this, most children will be able to identify with the changes that happen to the trees shown in the book by comparing them to the trees where they live. For those children who live where the leaves do not change color or fall to the ground, this story will help them visualize a greater variety of trees. Adapt the activities in this chapter based on the season and the types of trees common in your location.

Activities

FALL ACTIVITIES

1. In the fall, children will enjoy collecting leaves from various species of trees and from trees of various sizes and colors. Have children press these leaves between sheets of waxed paper and place them in a paper frame to make sunlight catchers (see fig. 6.1) or the "leafy heads" of imaginary characters that thrive in the fall.

Fig. 6.1. Sunlight Catcher.

2. Leaf rubbings of various tree leaves make splendid collages. Invite a "tree expert" to accompany the class on an expedition to gather leaves for making collages. Common deciduous trees include maple, oak, elm, birch, poplar, linden, beech, chestnut, mountain ash, ash, tulip, and sycamore. How can these trees be identified? What trees common to your location are not in this list? Use a tree identification guide to learn names of other trees that grow in your location. In what environment does each type of tree thrive?

3. Ask children why leaves change color, why leaves fall to the ground in autumn, and why evergreens stay green all winter. After children learn the answers to these questions, have them create a pantomime or a skit that portrays their knowledge.

   a. *Why do leaves change color?* Leaves change color because the sap in the tree has stopped flowing and chlorophyll is no longer being formed. Therefore, the green color is no longer present and other colors emerge.

   b. *Why do leaves fall to the ground in autumn?* Leaves fall to protect the tree during the heavy winter snows. If the leaves remained on the tree, the branches would break from the weight of the snow, and the tree would die.

   c. *Why do evergreens stay green all winter?* Their narrow "leaves" (needles) do not accumulate heavy amounts of snow. Therefore, an evergreen tree can survive the winter without shedding its leaves.

4. Have children make ink prints of various leaves. This can be done any time of the year that leaves are available and are not too dry and brittle. Use block printing ink and an inking roller (available at craft stores). Place ink on a board and roll it out thinly and evenly. Use the roller to apply ink to the leaf; pat the inked leaf onto paper or another surface. (Use waterproof ink to print leaves on T-shirts.) Or, have children print leaves of a favorite tree on writing paper and write a story about the tree.

5. In the fall, most trees drop seeds onto the ground. Gather a variety of seeds for children to study. How are they structured? How does the structure of each type of seed help its dispersal (e.g., a maple seed has two "winged" sides, allowing "flight" away from the tree). Dry some of the seeds. Have children draw outlines of geometric shapes on paper and fill in the spaces with seeds to make seed mosaics.

6. In the fall, forest trees bear many kinds of seeds (see fig. 6.2). On a nature walk, collect a variety of seeds, nuts, and cones. Open the seeds and have children examine the various structures that lie inside the protective coverings. Have children look inside the coverings for something that resembles a tiny plant. How would the seed be dispersed in nature? What conditions does the embryo need for growth?

7. Acorns are common in many parts of the country where oak trees grow. Using potting soil and Styrofoam cups, have children plant several acorns. Be sure to place them in direct sunlight and water them as they sprout and grow. NOTE: Acorns can cause sickness if ingested.

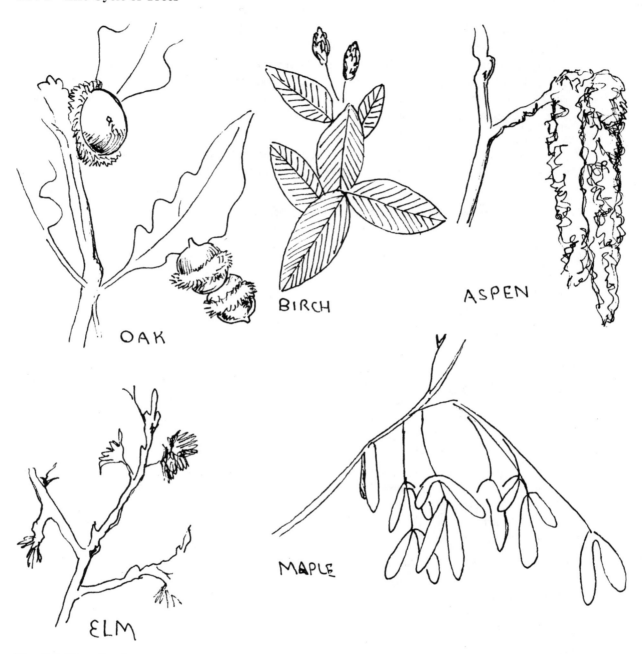

OAK

BIRCH

ASPEN

ELM

MAPLE

Fig. 6.2. Tree Seeds.

WINTER ACTIVITIES

8. In the winter, the leaves from deciduous trees fall to the ground. Evergreen trees, however, keep their needles. Gently remove small bunches of needles and cones from various kinds of evergreen trees for children to study in the classroom. Evergreen trees are classified by the number of needles in each bunch as well as by the shape of these needles and the kind of cones produced by the tree. Common varieties of evergreen include pine, hemlock, fir, and cedar (see fig. 6.3).

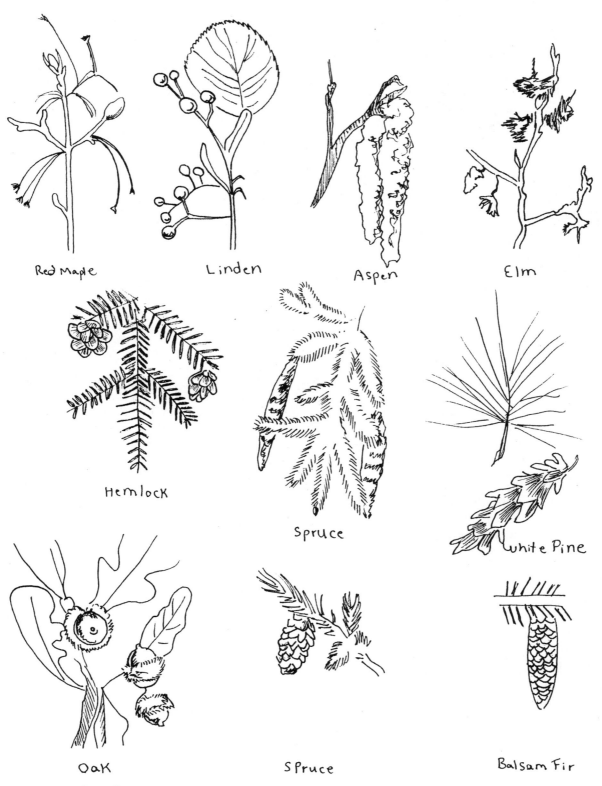

Fig. 6.3. Various Cones.

From *More Science Through Children's Literature.* © 1998 Butzow and Butzow. Teacher Ideas Press. (800) 237-6124.

9.   The bark of the deciduous tree becomes much more obvious in the winter because the leaves have fallen to the ground. Have children examine the bark from a variety of common trees. What words would they use to describe the various kinds of bark? Can the children now distinguish different kinds of trees by examining their bark rather than their leaves?

10.   Have children make bark rubbings (see fig. 6.4) by placing a sheet of paper on the bark and rubbing the surface with the side of a crayon. Hang the rubbings or use them as wrapping paper.

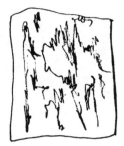 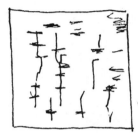 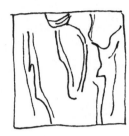 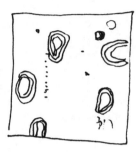

Fig. 6.4. Bark Rubbings.

11.   People often wait until the winter season to cut down trees. Ask children to think of reasons why someone would wait until it is cold and snowy to cut down a tree. Have children describe what they think it would be like to accompany someone on a tree-cutting expedition in the winter. Ask a library media specialist to help children find literature about people going out to cut down Christmas trees. Judith Hendershot's book *In Coal Country* depicts Christmas trees being cut down and taken home.

12.   Many familiar trees have a distinguishing silhouette. The shapes are called pyramidal, weeping, vase, globular, and columnar (see fig. 6.5). Have children compare these shapes to the shapes of trees in the schoolyard or in a nearby park. Using figure 6.5, have children make symmetrical paper cutouts of the five common shapes of trees to add to their leaf collages (see activity 2).

Fig. 6.5. Tree Shapes.

SPRING ACTIVITIES

13. In the spring, flowers and leaves begin to sprout on trees. Some flowers will eventually become fruit. Have children use a magnifying lens to examine buds and the various parts of the buds. Have children do this every few days to see the progress of the buds as they become leaves or flowers. NOTE: If possible, observe low-hanging branches, to avoid cutting or harming the trees.

14. In the spring, tree flowers produce pollen, which fertilizes the eggs in the tree flower to make the seeds grow. Have children study the pollen from a variety of trees with a magnifying lens. Each plant produces unique pollen. Have children draw the various pollen grains and consult an encyclopedia to learn more about pollen. NOTE: Before beginning this activity, ask children if they have allergies to pollen.

15. Spring is a good time to plant trees. Invite a person from a nearby nursery or home-and-garden center to visit the class and discuss the criteria for selecting a tree and the directions for planting it. To involve children in the management of the school, as well as in beautifying school grounds, help them organize a fund-raising event to collect money for buying and planting trees.

16. Seed catalogs are interesting and can help one decide what kind of tree to plant. Have children obtain addresses of various nurseries or tree centers by looking through the advertisements at the back of magazines for homemakers. Have children write and mail requests for seed catalogs. They may want to try this company:

    Musser Forests, Inc.
    P.O. Box 340
    Indiana, PA 15701-0340
    (412) 465-5685

ACTIVITIES FOR ANY SEASON

17. There are many reasons why people need trees. Have children list and illustrate these reasons.

18. The story *Red Leaf, Yellow Leaf* can be sung to the tune "Here We Go 'Round the Mulberry Bush." The following lyrics tell the life cycle of the sugar maple tree.

'Round and round the seeds are blown,
　　the seeds are blown,
　　the seeds are blown,
'Round and round the seeds are blown,
Early in the morning.
Seeds lie sleeping among the leaves,
　　among the leaves,
　　among the leaves,
Seeds lie sleeping among the leaves,
Early in the morning.
Seeds sprout roots and start to grow,
　　start to grow,
　　start to grow,
Seeds sprout roots and start to grow,
Early in the morning.
Tiny leaves unfold on stems,
　　unfold on stems,
　　unfold on stems,
Tiny leaves unfold on stems,
Early in the morning.
Nursery workers transplant the sprouts,
　　transplant the sprouts,
　　transplant the sprouts,
Nursery workers transplant the sprouts,
Early in the morning.
The roots are wrapped and tied with twine,
　　tied with twine,
　　tied with twine,
The roots are wrapped and tied with twine,
Early in the morning.
The trees go to the garden center,
　　the garden center,
　　the garden center,
The trees go to the garden center,
Early in the morning.

We bought a tree for Arbor Day,
　　for Arbor Day,
　　for Arbor Day,
We bought a tree for Arbor Day,
Early in the morning.
This is the way we dig a hole,
　　dig a hole,
　　dig a hole,
This is the way we dig a hole,
Early in the morning.
This is the way we cover the roots,
　　cover the roots,
　　cover the roots,
This is the way we cover the roots,
Early in the morning.
Trees hold treats for winter birds,
　　for winter birds,
　　for winter birds,
Trees hold treats for winter birds,
Early in the morning.
Summer is a time for growth,
　　time for growth,
　　time for growth,
Summer is a time for growth,
Early in the morning.
Seeds have formed and leaves fall off,
　　leaves fall off,
　　leaves fall off,
Seeds have formed and leaves fall off,
Early in the morning.
The tree will live for many years,
　　many years,
　　many years,
The tree will live for many years,
And bring us lots of joy.

19. As a celebration for children's year-long association with trees and the life cycle of trees, plant a tree (see fig. 6.6)! This might be done in conjunction with an Arbor Day celebration. To obtain information about Arbor Day, write to:

National Arbor Day Foundation
100 Arbor Avenue
Nebraska City, NE 68410
(402) 474-5655
www.arborday.org

NOTE: Arbor Day is designated as the last Friday in April. However, each state usually sets their own day to coincide with the optimum planting time. This date ranges from early December to late May.

20. Have children make costumes from old clothes and hats, or wear paper masks, and reenact the life cycle of a tree as portrayed in *Red Leaf, Yellow Leaf*.

Fig. 6.6. Planting a Tree.

Related Books and References

Cohen, Michael R., and Charles R. Barman. "Did You Notice the Color of Trees in the Spring?" *Science and Children* 31, no. 5 (February 1994): 20–22.

Dobey, Daniel C. "Wah Da' (The Maple)." *Science Scope* 19, no. 1 (September 1995): 20–23.

Ehlert, Lois. *Eating the Alphabet: Fruits and Vegetables from A to Z*. San Diego, CA: Harcourt Brace Jovanovich, 1989.

———. *Planting a Rainbow*. San Diego, CA: Harcourt Brace Jovanovich, 1988.

Geisel, Theodore (Dr. Seuss). *The Lorax*. New York: Random House, 1971.

Hendershot, Judith. *In Coal Country*. New York: Alfred A. Knopf, 1987.

Nelson, Don. "Sizing Up Trees." *Science and Children* 32, no. 8 (May 1995): 16–18.

Srulowitz, Frances. "Diary of a Tree." *Science and Children* 29, no. 5 (February 1992): 19–21.

Vivaldi, Antonio. *The Four Seasons*. English Chamber Orchestra. Nigel Kennedy.

Chapter 7

The Desert

Cactus Hotel

by Brenda Guiberson
New York: Henry Holt, 1991

Summary

Everyone wants to live in the Cactus Hotel because it yields protection from extreme heat and cold, as well as from predatory animals of the desert. This "hotel," which is the name given to a saguaro cactus, lives more than 200 years, and even when decomposing, it continues to serve as a hotel for desert creatures.

Science and Content Related Concepts

Desert ecology, cactus life cycle, microclimates, seed dispersal

Content Related Words

Saguaro, cactus, Arizona, pollination, nectar

Activities

1. This story takes place in the Sonoran desert of Arizona. Using an atlas or road map, have children locate Arizona, the city of Tucson, the Saguaro National Monuments, and the Sonoran desert. NOTE: Have available several maps, because not all of these points of interest are found on every map. However, children will still be able to form an impression of the locale of this story by locating the city and state where the story takes place.

2. Seed dispersal is one of the most important themes discussed in this story. To help gather seeds from wild plants for observation, have children stuff an old sock with crumpled newspaper. Tie the top of the sock, leaving a few feet of string to use as a handle (see fig. 7.1). Drag the sock for 25 to 30 feet through an area that has been mowed. Check the sock for seeds and put them into a container. Repeat the dragging several times. As children gather seeds, have them observe the plants that dropped them. How do the plants shed their seeds for dispersal? Have children examine the seeds using a magnifying lens and classify them into categories (e.g., "winged" seeds, "stick-tight" seeds). NOTE: This activity works best in a weeded location but can also be done on a cultivated lawn.

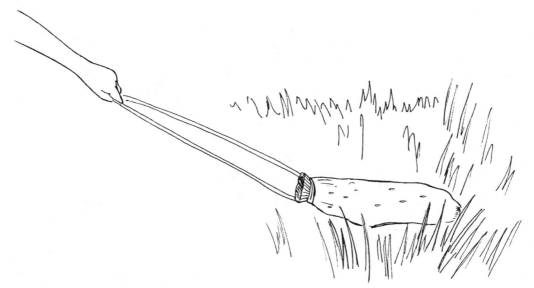

Fig. 7.1. Gathering Seeds.

3. If it is not possible to gather seeds outdoors, have children examine seeds that are commonly found in the home—spices, such as mustard and celery seed— or found in fruits and vegetables available at a supermarket. Have children deduce how these seeds were dropped from the plant in nature. In the case of fruits and vegetables, have children describe or draw the trees or plants that produced the seeds. Encyclopedias or plant and garden books will help children with this task.

4. The children can study fruits and vegetables from a supermarket. Have them ask themselves questions about why the plant produces a fruit or vegetable. What adaptation for seed dispersal does the fruit or vegetable provide? Who or what will disperse these seeds? How is the dispersal accomplished? NOTE: Fruits, such as coconut, are actually the seed. Other fruits, such as peaches, cover their seeds; when humans or animals eat the fruit, the seeds are exposed.

5. After children have studied seeds and seed dispersal, have them invent a picture of a seed and seedpod. Remind them that the seed must be protected somehow by the pod and the plant. Challenge children to invent seeds that have these characteristics:

Floats on water

Sticks to a passing animal

Passes through an animal's digestive system

Floats great distances in the wind

Glides to a new location

Attracts the eye of an animal or bird

Shoots away from the parent plant

Dropped by a bird as it flies

6. After sharing the children's drawings about seeds and how they have adapted to different situations, ask children why it is important that seeds be dispersed. Why are there so many sizes and shapes of seeds? What conditions must occur for seeds to germinate? Will all seeds that germinate continue to grow to maturity? Why?

7. Seeds do not always germinate when they are planted, and some germinate slower than others. The germination rate can be controlled to some degree, however. Have children fill small pots or dishes with potting soil, then plant seeds under various conditions:

   Watered heavily every day

   Not watered at all

   Watered lightly every other day

   Soaked in water before planting

   Placed in direct sunlight

   Placed in the shade

   Placed in a cold place

   Placed in a hot place

   If desired, have children combine these conditions to create more variables (e.g., heavily watered plants in the sunlight, heavily watered plants in the shade, no water in hot places, no water in cold places). Have children label their pots. NOTE: Use fast-sprouting seeds, such as alfalfa, radish, mustard, celery, or bean seeds, when working with young children.

   Once the seeds are sprouted, have children conclude which condition, or which combination of variables, produced the fastest germination and healthiest-looking plant (see activity 8 for judging criteria). Children should consider these variables:

   Amount of water used

   Temperature of the surrounding air

   Amount of sunlight exposure

8. Assign children to monitor specific seed pots. As the seeds begin to sprout, have children make a pictorial log of their plants as they appear each day for one to two weeks. Children should observe the height of the plant, number of leaves, development and shape of the leaves, color of the leaves and stem, strength of the stem, effects of watering, and overall health of the plant. Continue the experiment as the plants grow or have children transplant the healthy plants into gardens or larger pots for classroom viewing. NOTE: Activities 7 and 8 give the children the opportunity to see continuity of life by tracing the life of a plant from seed to maturity.

9. Have each child create a flower from modeling clay. Place a small amount of dusting powder into the center of the flower to simulate the pollen on the reproductive parts of the plant. Have children design and make a bird, insect, or animal using colored pipe cleaners, and show how it might gather or disperse pollen from the flower. Observe how much pollen sticks to the creature. Compare how the pollen sticks to each bird, insect, or animal as children share their work with each another. Which flowers are best suited for dispersing pollen in this manner? Which of the birds, insects, and animals are able to most effectively gather or disperse pollen?

10. Bats are essential to the life of the saguaro cactus because they pollinate the saguaro's flowers. Reread to children the book *Stellaluna*. Have children write to the Bat Conservation International for more information about these animals; the address is included in "Chapter 5," activity 1.

11. Plants must adapt to their environment to survive. Cacti are able to live where few other plants do because they have adapted to life in hot, arid climates. Have children simulate how a cactus retains large amounts of water in its arms and stem: Place sponges on a shallow baking tray (see fig. 7.2); slowly add water to the tray until the sponges become saturated and no standing water is left. Discuss how the sponges reacted to the addition of the water. Set the tray in sunlight for a day and check the amount of moisture in the sponges every two hours. How long does it take for the sponges to dry? How does this relate to the cactus, which absorbs enormous amounts of water from the ground during a rainstorm? How and when does the cactus use this stored water? What is the appearance of the cactus at different stages during this process?

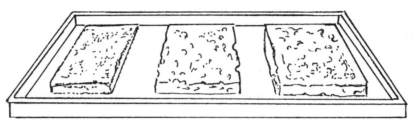

Fig. 7.2. Sponges.

12. Observing a desert landscape, one will probably not see any animal life despite the fact that thousands of species make a home in the desert. Ask children where the animals would be found. Are animals able to camouflage themselves and blend into the landscape? How do animals depend on plants and other animals for protection from the elements or from predators? What special microclimates exist in the desert that allow plants and animals to live there even though they cannot tolerate extremes of temperature and sunlight?

13. The desert is extremely hot in the daytime, yet night temperatures are much lower than those of the daytime. Ask children why the sand is hot during the day. Is it cooler at night? Have children try this experiment:

   a. Obtain three small, heat-resistant dishes. Put one inch of soil into the first dish. Put one inch of sand into the second dish. Put one inch of room-temperature water into the third dish.

   b. Shine a heat lamp onto the three dishes (see fig. 7.3). Measure and record the temperature of the soil, the sand, and the water every 2 minutes for 10 minutes. NOTE: Caution children not to touch the heat lamp during or after the activity.

   c. Turn off the heat lamp but continue to measure and record the temperature of the three samples every 2 minutes for 10 minutes.

   d. Discuss the results: Which material heated fastest? Which heated slowest? Which cooled fastest? Which cooled slowest? How does this experiment relate to the desert sand and climate? What can be inferred about the behavior of desert animals? Where would they most likely live? During what part of the day would they most likely be active? How does this experiment relate to human beings and their lives (i.e., where they live, the clothes they wear)?

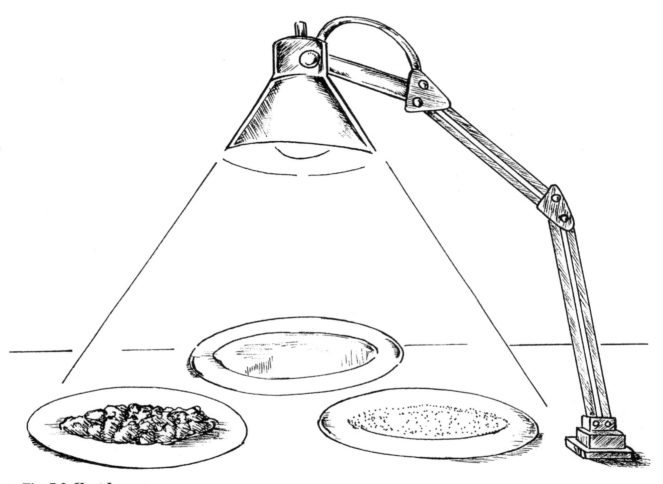

Fig. 7.3. Heat Lamps.

14. Moisture, temperature, and sunlight affect human beings, as well as plants and animals. In the classroom, have children predict which areas of the school playground or schoolyard are wet or dry, hot or cool, light or dark. Divide the class into three teams and go outside. Have each group test their predictions for each of the three variables. Were their predictions correct? Why do some living things need sunlight to thrive? Why do some need shade? What happens when plants or animals are too long in the sunlight or shade? How can people protect themselves against sunlight? Can people get too much shade? How do humans change their environment by manipulating moisture, temperature, and sunlight (e.g., the area near an air conditioner might be quite different than the area near a sunny window)?

15. Animals often live in or about trees. If there is a tree on the school playground or nearby, have children try to observe animals that live in or about the trees. Children may have to do this at a distance, using binoculars or videotape, because animals are frightened by noise and the presence of people. How do animals live in the trees? What role do animals play in seed dispersal? Do animals contribute anything to their environment (e.g., acorns are dispersed by squirrels, thus ensuring the growth of new oak trees)? Do the animals harm their environment in any way?

16. The fallen cactus is still useful as a home for myriad insects and small animals. In this way, the cactus is much like the rotting log of the forest. Obtain a rotting log for children to examine. First, have them observe the entire log; then have them use a magnifying lens to observe smaller creatures. Capture any such creatures in a jar for a brief observation period, then release the animals unharmed. NOTE: It may be more appropriate to do this activity outdoors. Or, keep the rotting log—or pieces of a rotting log—in a covered terrarium in the classroom for a few days for examination.

17. Have children pretend that they are old saguaro cacti that have lived many years in the desert. Have them tell a young animal or insect visitor what it is like to be a "cactus hotel."

18. Have each child select an animal from the list of words used in activity 21 and write a short report about the animal. Have the child include a drawing of the animal. Hang the reports and drawings on a bulletin board or in a school hallway.

19. Some children may want to research cacti and desert flowers for the bulletin board display. Have a library media specialist help children find books on these topics. Have children write informational pieces on and draw pictures of their featured plants.

20. Read aloud to children the story *Roxaboxen* by Alice McLerran, which takes place in a desert environment much like the one in *Cactus Hotel*.

21. Word Scramble—Animals of the Arizona Desert

Many animals live in the desert. Names of several of these animals are given below in scrambled form. Use the accompanying clues to unscramble the words.

CLUES

a. I am known for my bark. I am about the size of a dog but can run 40 miles per hour. _____ _____ (yoceto)

b. I have a long curved tail that arches over my body. I am a poisonous arachnid and will kill any relatives I happen to meet. _____ (nocsorip)

c. I am a reptile that can hiss, but I am harmless to human beings. If I lose my tail in a fight, I can grow a new one. _____ (aildzr)

d. I am a reptile and have no legs. I have scaly skin and swallow my prey whole. _____ _____ (knesa)

e. I can rest easily on the side of a tree when I eat insects. I have a strong beak and a long tongue, which helps me eat my prey. _____ (dooperweck)

f. I am as short as $\frac{1}{16}$ of an inch or as long as two inches. I have jaws made for fighting, eating, and carrying things. _____ (nat)

g. I can spin sticky webs to catch my prey. I have eight legs and could possibly be poisonous to humans. _____ (ripsed)

h. I am related to cardinals, grosbecks, and sparrows. I am well loved by farmers because I eat insects. _____ (chinf)

i. I am a chattering rodent that lives in the trunk of a tree. I am related to some species of animals that can fly. _____ (rersquil)

j. I can survive anywhere in the world and am known as a sign of peace. I am most closely related to a pigeon. _____ (veod)

k. I am the smallest of all birds but have a long beak. My wings make a distinctive sound. _____ _____ (mindgumbrih)

l. I am a venomous lizard. I grow to 21 inches in length and live in rivers in Arizona. _____ _____ (agil retnoms)

m. I resemble a dog, but I can burrow into the ground. I am sometimes red or gray, and I can play dead when there is a predator near. _____ (xfo)

n. I look like a mouse, but I am a flying mammal. I have an exceptionally keen sense of hearing. _____ (tab)

o. I am very unlike the cartoon character with my name. I live in the southwestern United States and in Mexico. _____ (doarnurenr)

p. I am about four inches long, though my tail, alone, is about three inches in length. I am not a rat. I am known for eating crops. _____ (usome)

q. I have long, needle-like talons to hold my prey. I am a nocturnal animal that eats small mice. _____ (low)

r. I have long ears and a bushy tail. I collect bits of materials for my den and make my nests from cacti. _____ (crapakt)

s. I am born with my eyes open and begin to hop around shortly after birth. I must avoid the mammals, birds, and reptiles that consider me their prey. _____ (ticakbabjr)

WORDS USED

ant	hummingbird	roadrunner
bat	jackrabbit	scorpion
coyote	lizard	snake
dove	mouse	spider
finch	owl	squirrel
fox	packrat	woodpecker
gila monster		

Related Books and References

Cannon, Janell. *Stellaluna*. San Diego, CA: Harcourt Brace Jovanovich, 1993.

Evans, Doris. "So, This Is the Desert." *Science Scope* 18, no. 6 (March 1995): 36–39.

Grofe, Ferde. *The Grand Canyon Suite*. New York Philharmonic Orchestra. Leonard Bernstein.

Kepler, Lynne. "Saguaro Science." *Science and Children* 30, no. 7 (August 1993): 42.

McLerran, Alice. *Roxaboxen*. Illustrated by Barbara Cooney. New York: Puffin Books, 1992.

Vesilind, Prit J. "Anything but Empty: The Sonoran Desert." *National Geographic* 186, no. 3 (September 1994): 37–63.

Chapter 8

The Rain Forest

The Great Kapok Tree

by Lynne Cherry
San Diego, CA: Harcourt Brace Jovanovich, 1990

Summary

From the bottom of the rain forest's dark understory to the top of its bright canopy rises the giant kapok tree. It houses its own community of creatures and is but one of the species that must be saved, along with all inhabitants of the rain forest.

Science and Content Related Concepts

Rain forest, environment, conservation, balance of nature, interdependence, slash-and-burn agriculture

Content Related Words

Canopy, understory, forest floor, community, pollinate, camouflage, epiphytes

Activities

1. Have children construct a rain forest in the classroom by making trees out of mailing tubes and construction paper (see fig. 8.1). Large sheets of paper can be used to include the animals and plants featured in the book, as well as other rain forest inhabitants that children discover using additional sources. Have a library media specialist help children locate books about the rain forest to assist them with research. If possible, keep these books on a shelf in the classroom during this unit.

2. After constructing a classroom rain forest, visit a local zoo, if one is nearby. Have children study and note the habitats of the animals that are indigenous to the rain forest. If going to a zoo is not possible, have children use videos and print media to obtain information about these animals.

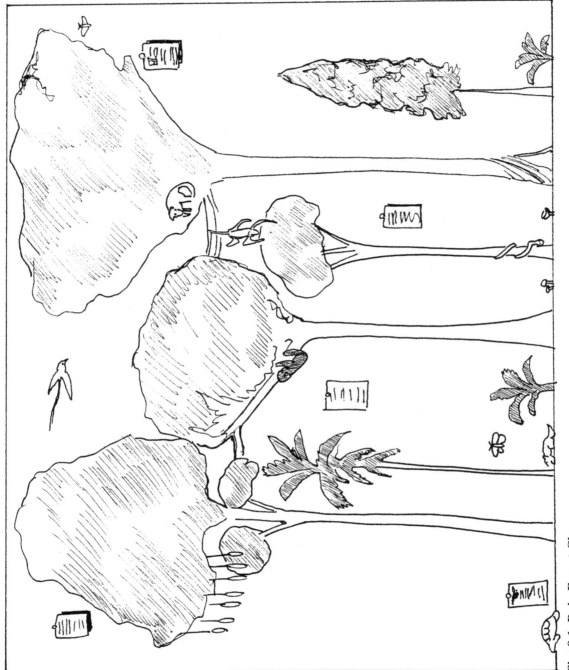

Fig. 8.1. Rain Forest Classroom.

3. Have each child "adopt" an animal or plant from the rain forest and write a report about it. The report should include a drawing and the following information:

   Description

   Habitat

   Source of nourishment

   Means of protection from predators, including humans

   Specific adaptations of the animal or plant

   Interdependence with other animals or plants

4. Hang children's reports about their adopted animals in the classroom rain forest in appropriate places (i.e., the canopy, the understory, the forest floor). Invite parents, visitors, and other students to visit and discuss how the classroom rain forest depicts the real rain forest.

5. Camouflage is of utmost importance to the animals of the rain forest. Have each child select a place in the classroom rain forest where they would like to hide an "animal" they make. Using potatoes or rocks, along with paints, scraps of material, construction paper, yarn, etc., have children make and camouflage their animals (see fig. 8.2). The teacher must provide a time for children to hide their animals when there is little chance others will observe the hiding place. Invite children to find the animals after they have been hidden.

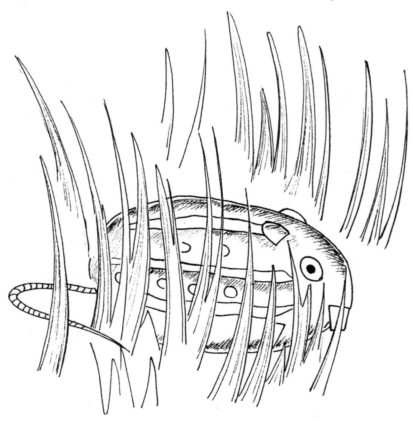

Fig. 8.2. Hidden Animals.

6. As an ongoing project throughout this unit, have children grow plants. Many common house plants actually originated in the rain forest. Ask personnel at a floral shop or nursery to recommend plants that would best represent the rain forest. Ferns and vines and plants known as *epiphytes* (e.g., orchids) are likely candidates.

7. Have children play a matching game to help them learn more about the animals of the rain forest. The animals included are the three-toed sloth, anteater, howler monkey, boa constrictor, jaguar, tarantula, army ant, vampire bat, piranha, toucan, tree frog, and bee. Two clues are included for each animal—24 clues in all. Write each clue on an index card and pass out the cards to children. The challenge is for each child to find another child with a clue for the same animal. In other words, two children will have a clue for the same animal but must conclude what that animal is through reasoning and background knowledge. Do not list animal names on the index cards. NOTE: Adjust the number of clues provided to accommodate the size of the class.

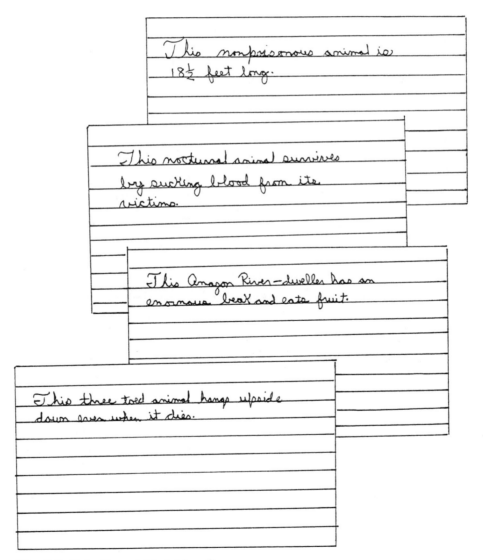

Fig. 8.3. Rain Forest Matching Game.

THREE-TOED SLOTH

a. This three-toed animal hangs upside down, even when it dies.

b. This 12-pound animal is the slowest animal on Earth, moving at a rate of one mile in 15 hours.

ANTEATER

a. This seven-foot-long animal can eat 35,000 ants in one day.

b. This animal has a 22-inch-long tongue that it can flick into an anthill at a rate of 160 times per minute.

HOWLER MONKEY

a. This noisy animal is the largest primate in the New World.

b. This animal has a prehensile tail with which it can grab and hold things.

BOA CONSTRICTOR

a. This nonpoisonous animal is $18\frac{1}{2}$ feet long.

b. This slow-moving animal crushes its prey to death.

JAGUAR

a. This big cat is six feet long and can weigh up to 250 pounds.

b. Black and tan spots help camouflage this endangered animal, which is prized for its coat.

TARANTULA

a. This hairy animal has eight legs and lives on the forest floor.

b. Although the bite of this creature is generally harmless, it was once thought to cause its victims to dance madly.

ARMY ANT

a. This insect marches with others of its kind in straight lines up to one mile in length.

b. This insect eats spiders, lizards, and centipedes, among other things, and communicates by releasing a chemical from its body.

VAMPIRE BAT

a. This flying mammal lives in groups and weighs only half an ounce.

b. This nocturnal animal survives by sucking blood from its victims.

PIRANHA

a. This fish can strip down its prey to a skeleton in a matter of seconds.

b. This flesh-eating animal with razor-sharp teeth hunts in groups called schools.

TOUCAN

a. This Amazon River dweller has an enormous beak and eats fruit.

b. This bird can be brilliantly colored with red, yellow, orange, green, blue, white, and black.

TREE FROG

a. Before reaching adulthood, this animal exists as an egg and a tadpole.

b. This one-inch amphibian has a vocal pouch on its throat.

BEE

a. This insect has six legs, three body parts, two antennae, and two pairs of wings.

b. This insect helps to pollinate flowers as it gathers nectar to make honey.

8. The soils of the rain forest are being washed away as trees, such as mahogany and teak are cut down and, therefore, no longer hold the earth in place. To demonstrate for children the effects of water erosion, make two hills of firmly packed dirt, each on a large plate (see fig. 8.4). On one hill, plant grass seed or small plants. After the plants are established, begin watering the two hills of soil every day, using the same amount of water on each hill. Do this for one week. Have children observe the differences between the plant-covered hill and the hill with no plants. What can they conclude about erosion in the rain forest? Can erosion be stopped? Where else might erosion occur? Are there other kinds of erosion?

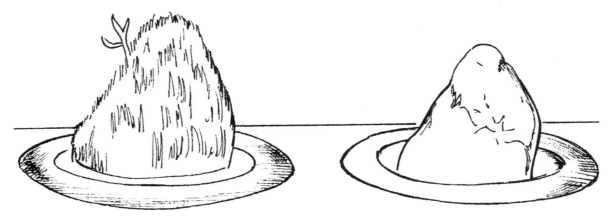

Fig. 8.4. Erosion Plates.

9. Slash-and-burn agriculture—clearing land for agriculture or cattle grazing—is another cause of erosion. Discuss with children how this practice contributes to soil and wind erosion. NOTE: Rain forest soil is infertile and cannot support crops for more than a few years. After this, the soil is depleted and new land must be cleared.

10. Discuss with children how slash-and-burn agriculture affects the quality of the air in the rain forest. How are plants, animals, and humans affected by this practice? NOTE: Smoke from slash-and-burn agriculture causes air pollution, as well as a release of carbon dioxide into the air. The carbon dioxide is trapped in Earth's atmosphere and contributes to the greenhouse effect.

11. Discuss with children predator-prey relationships. Remind children that most animals prey on smaller animals for food. Each animal, thereby, becomes prey for a larger animal. Are human beings considered predators or prey? How are predator-prey relationships and the food chain, or the balance of nature, related? What happens if this balance changes (e.g., if a certain species becomes extinct)?

12. Rain forests exist in the United States in Alaska, Hawaii, Washington state, and the Virgin Islands. The Washington state rain forest is protected from exploitation by being part of the Olympic National Park and the Olympic National Forest. The Olympic National Park and National Forest include the valleys of the Quinault, Hoh, and Queets rivers. Have children study a map of this area. What can they conclude about Washington, its residents, its geography, and its plant life? What comparisons and contrasts to your state, or to other parts of Washington, can be made? What can be concluded and predicted for your state,

or for other parts of Washington? Have children research other U.S. rain forests and compare them to Washington's rain forest, as well as to other rain forests throughout the world.

13. Have children design and write an advertisement for radio, television, or print media that calls attention to the plight of the rain forest and its inhabitants. Have children use information they have learned from this unit. For more information, have children access the Internet and search it using the term *rain forest*. This search will provide many sources of information and help you use material that is easily understood by other children (e.g., "Every year, an area of the rain forest the size of Pennsylvania is destroyed"). Have children share their advertisements with others at school.

14. Chico Mendes is known as a hero of the rain forest. Have a library media specialist help children find information about this man, who was murdered on December 22, 1988, for his activist beliefs and demonstrations against the abuses of the rain forest.

15. To learn more about the rain forest, have children write to these sources:

> The Nature Conservancy
> Adopt-an-Acre Program
> 1815 N. Lynn Street
> Arlington, VA 22209
> (703) 841-8771
> www.tnc.org

> Rain Forest Alliance
> Suite 512
> 270 Lafayette Street
> New York, NY 10012
> (212) 677-1900; (212) 941-1900
> www.rainforest-alliance.org

> World Wildlife Fund
> 1250 24th Street NW
> Washington, DC 20037
> (202) 293-4800
> www.wwf.org

16. Have children conclude this unit with these two "tasty" activities:

   a. Give each child a chocolate chip cookie and a toothpick. The challenge is to remove the chocolate chips with the toothpick but leave the cookie intact (see fig. 8.5). Children quickly learn that this is impossible. Discuss how this activity can be an analogy for harvesting trees from the rain forest: Trees cannot be continuously harvested from the rain forest without risk of destroying the rain forest, itself.

   b. Environmentally sound ways of using the rain forest are being advocated. One proposal is that only renewable resources could be harvested from the rain forest, which would preclude harvesting trees or otherwise destroying the forest floor. Have children make a tasty treat using ingredients harvested or made from renewable products of the rain forest:

Fig. 8.5. Mining for a Chocolate Chip.

1 cup peanuts
1 cup cashews
1 cup banana chips
1 cup chocolate chips
1 cup dried pineapple chunks
1 cup flaked coconut

Mix all ingredients and enjoy.

17. *The Amazon Trail* is a computer simulation game available from MECC, similar in nature to the well-known *The Oregon Trail*. For more information about this product, contact:

MECC (Minnesota Educational Computing Consortium)
6160 Summit Drive, N.
Minneapolis, MN 55430-4003
www.macfaq.com/faq/vender/software/677.html

Related Books and References

Andrews, Julia L. *Jungles and Rain Forests*. New York: Trumpet Club, 1991.

Munn, Charles A. "Winged Rainbows: Macaws." *National Geographic* 185, no. 1 (January 1994): 118–40.

VanDyk, Jere. "Amazon: South American's River Road." *National Geographic* 187, no. 2 (February 1995): 3–39.

Villa-Lobos, Heitor. *Bachianas Brazilieras*. Mexico City Philharmonic Orchestra. Hector Batiz.

Wilson, Edward O. "Rain Forest Canopy: The High Frontier." *National Geographic* 180, no. 6 (December 1991): 78–107.

Part II
Earth and Space Sciences

Chapter 9

Erosion and Stratification

The Sun, the Wind, and the Rain

by Lisa Westberg Peters
New York: Henry Holt, 1988

Summary

Elizabeth's mountain at the beach was much like the real mountains that she would see. Both were built in layers over time, but the most important resemblance was the effect on both mountains of the Sun, the wind, and the rain.

Science and Content Related Concepts

Composition of the earth, passage of time, stratification of the earth, effect of weather on the earth, erosion

Content Related Words

Geology, rocks, mountains, canyons, oceans, sandstone, environment, eons

Activities

1. Have children use a small wading pool as a base for making their own mountain. Empty several bags of sand into the wading pool until a mountain, like Elizabeth's, is formed. Children should shape a peak for the mountain using small amounts of water (e.g., using a plant mister or spray bottle). Have children try the following experiments and photograph the results:

    a. Shine a heat lamp onto the mountain for about an hour. What happens to the mountain? What can children conclude about the effect of the Sun on the earth? NOTE: Caution children not to touch the heat lamp during or after the activity.

    b. Using a gentle fan, blow air onto the mountain. Stand several feet away from the mountain and observe the effect. What can children conclude about the effect of the wind on the earth? What would happen if the speed of the fan was increased? NOTE: Do not allow children to increase the speed of the fan because sand might be blown into their eyes.

c. Gently pour water onto the mountain until the effects of water erosion can be seen. What can children conclude about the effect of water on the earth?

Have children discuss the effects of heat, wind, and water on their mountain. Can children find pictures in *The Sun, the Wind and the Rain* that show the effects of erosion on Elizabeth's mountain, as well as the real mountain? NOTE: If possible, use different kinds or colors of sand to build the mountain. Children will see the various layers, or strata, appear as the mountain erodes.

Fig. 9.1. Building a Mountain.

2. Have children prepare a photographic essay that tells the story of the class making the mountain in a wading pool and simulating the forces of nature. Display the essay on a classroom bulletin board.

3. If possible, arrange a field trip to a place where children can see the strata of the earth. Strata can usually be seen in places where a highway has been cut through layers of rock. An old quarry, if safe, can also reveal many layers of rock. If this is not possible, photograph (or have a parent photograph) these areas. Add these pictures to the bulletin board display from activity 2.

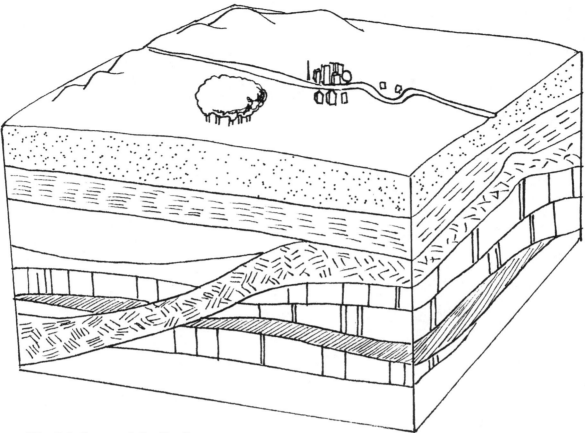

Fig. 9.2. Strata of the Earth.

During the field trip, have children observe the strata of the earth. Are all layers, or strata, the same thickness? Do the strata lie perfectly flat? Are there places where a particular stratum disappears? How do the strata compare to one another in color? In texture and hardness? Generally, how can age of strata, in relation to one another, be determined? Which stratum is the oldest? Which stratum is the youngest? Are there places where older strata are found on top of younger strata? If so, how can children account for this? How do geologists determine the age of strata? Are animal fossils present in some of the strata? What can children conclude about animal shapes from their fossils? NOTE: A children's book about geology can help answer these questions. Books about dinosaurs and fossils may also be helpful as children learn about the history of Earth. Have children look for such books in the library media center.

4. To depict the concept of stratification artistically, have children fill clear, plastic cups with different-colored layers of sand. NOTE: To avoid mixing the layers, children should not shake or bump the cups.

5. Ask children how the layers of sand in the cup (from activity 5) are related to the strata of the earth. Have children gently insert a toothpick into the sand in their cup, along the inside of the cup (see fig. 9.3). The layers will be forced downward and fault-like impressions will form in the sand. What else can children do to influence the position of the layers?

What happens to strata when forces of nature (e.g., volcanic activity, earthquakes) disturb the earth? Over time, what things can affect strata? NOTE: To add texture to the strata, use various granular-type dry foods instead of sand (e.g., cornmeal, salt, flour, nutty cereal).

Fig. 9.3. Creating a Fault.

6. Sands and soils come in myriad textures and colors. Have children fill a tall, clear bottle with layers of various colors and textures of sands and soils. To obtain a large sampling, have children write to friends and relatives throughout the United States, asking them for about a cup of one type of sand or soil. Have children compare and contrast the various colors and textures. NOTE: Children may want to begin pen pal relationships if they will be writing to other children.

7. Obtain an inexpensive soil test kit and have children determine the contents of various soils. Have children test the soils around the school building or in nearby flower beds.

8. Have children simulate the strata of the earth using flattened pieces of Play Doh or other modeling clay. Build two separate, layered piles using various colors of clay. Have children gently push together the two piles (see fig. 9.4). The result will be an upheaval of the various layers, which simulates the way forces of nature can bring about changes in the earth. NOTE: This activity can also be done using two pieces of a candy bar that is made with layers of ingredients.

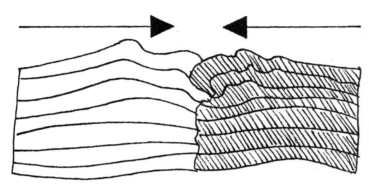

Fig. 9.4. Clay Stratification.

9. To observe how stratification of the earth occurs in water, have children fill a one-quart glass bottle with layers of various sizes of gravel and a sampling of various soils. Add water to the bottle until all of the layers are submerged (see fig. 9.5). Tightly place the cap on the bottle; turn the bottle upside down, then rightside up, several times. Let the contents of the bottle settle. The various strata will filter themselves into natural layers. What can children conclude about the material that settled at the bottom of the bottle? How does the bottom layer compare to the top layer? How would children describe the progression of materials from bottom to top? If children were to turn the bottle upside down, what would happen? Why? Have children verify whether their hypothesis was correct.

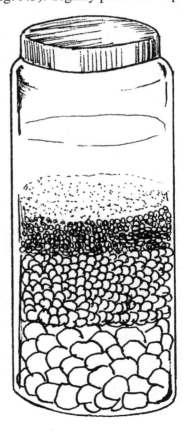

10. Many industries are dependent upon extracting various deposits from the earth, including coal, limestone, and gravel. Ask a library media specialist to help children determine if these industries exist in your community or if they once existed, but are now obsolete. If these industries do not exist in your community, have children use the library media center to research them. If possible, interview members of the community who were or are involved in these industries. What can children conclude about the earth from the presence of layers of coal, limestone, and gravel? For what purposes are coal, limestone, and gravel used? How are they extracted from the ground? How was extraction carried out before gasoline-powered engines were invented?

Fig. 9.5. Sediment Bottle.

11. A person who digs wells for a living—someone who knows much about the layers of the earth—is a "well driver." Invite a well driver to speak to the class about digging wells. Have children ask questions, such as: What strata of rock, soil, and sand are found in this area? Are these strata flat and even, or do they show the action of upheavals in the earth? What materials are used to drill through these strata? How deep must the well be to reach water? Would wells in various places in the community be the same, or do the strata vary by location? How does the depth of the water vary from place to place? How do well drivers know where to dig? Based on what children learn, have them draw and label a diagram of the strata present in your area.

12. Have children write an essay about how various forces (e.g., rain storms, wind storms, hurricanes, tornadoes, floods, volcanoes, earthquakes) contribute to shaping a mountain. Remind children to think about the real mountain and Elizabeth's sand mountain as they write the essay.

13. Based on their essays from activity 13, have children choreograph an interpretive dance that shows the effects on the Earth of the Sun, wind, water, and geologic upheavals.

14. Many folktales are cultural explanations of a natural phenomena. For example, tales were often told about spirits and creatures who lived high in the mountains where people had not ventured. (See, for example, "The Giant and the Four Winds," http://www.indians.org//welker.fourwind.htm.)

15. Have children write a folktale to explain a natural phenomenon (e.g., related to mountains, oceans, deserts). Mountains are formed by geologic activity within the Earth. Have children review what they have learned in this unit about how mountains are formed. Have children locate the following mountains on a relief map of the United States: Appalachian Mountains, Ozark Mountains, Rocky Mountains, Sierra Nevada Mountains, and Cascade Mountains. Have children notice other mountain ranges and locate mountain ranges in your area. Do children know which mountains are the oldest and which are the youngest? NOTE: If possible, do this activity with the aid of a molded relief map (a three-dimensional map on which scale elevation is portrayed).

16. Ask children if they have noticed how the temperature decreases when climbing a mountain. Have children try this challenging math activity about mountains: Outside of weather factors, the temperature decreases 6 degrees for every 1,000-foot increase in altitude. If one is at an elevation of 3,000 feet and the temperature is 50 degrees Fahrenheit, what will the temperature be at 6,000 feet? If one is at an elevation of 10,000 feet and the temperature is 40 degrees Fahrenheit, what will the temperature be at 4,000 feet? Have children write their own math story problems about temperature and elevation for other children to solve.

17. Word Scramble—Geology
    Geologic terms are given below in scrambled form. Use the accompanying clues to unscramble the words.

CLUES

a. Planet where we live _____ (raeht)

b. Landform higher than a hill _____ (unationm)

c. These objects were once hot and soft or liquid inside Earth _____ (kcor)

d. Change from one position to another _____ (fthis)

e. Process of wearing away, usually by wind or water _____ (serioon)

f. Deep cracks in Earth's surface that have steep, cliff walls _____ (scanoyn)

g. Long, narrow lowland between hills or ranges of mountains _____ (leyavl)

h. Extensive, level, treeless area of land _____ (nipal)

i. Layer of rock or soil _____ (tatursm)

j. It falls to the earth and can wear away rocks or soil _____ (nair)

WORDS USED

canyons	plain	shift
Earth	rain	stratum
erosion	rock	valley
mountain		

From More Science Through Children's Literature. © 1998 Butzow and Butzow. Teacher Ideas Press. (800) 237-6124.

18. Word Ladder—Erosion

First, match the words to the clues. Write the words in the puzzle blanks, which are formed around the word *erosion*.

CLUES

1. Where we live

2. It waters the earth

3. Top layer of land that can be washed away by wind or rain

4. Final destination of running water

5. It blows away particles of soil

6. It freezes in the cracks of the mountain and breaks the rock

7. Heat from here can crack rocks

WORDS USED

Earth	snow	Sun
rain	soil	wind
sea		

Fig. 9.6. Word Ladder—Erosion.

Related Books and References

Cole, Joanna. *The Magic School Bus Inside the Earth*. New York: Scholastic, 1987.

Colegate, Carol, and Janice Smith. "A Cave of Our Own." *Science and Children* 33, no. 1 (September 1995): 21–23.

Denver, John. *Rocky Mountain High*. RCA 5190.

Gore, Rick. "Living with California's Faults." *National Geographic* 187, no. 4 (April 1995): 2–35.

Lauber, Patricia. *Volcano: The Eruption and Healing of Mount St. Helens*. New York: Bradbury Press, 1986.

Lowder, Connie C. "Spelunking in the Classroom." *Science and Children* 31, no. 3 (November/December 1993): 19–22.

Sexton, Ursula. "Science Learning in the Sand." *Science and Children* 34, no. 4 (January 1997): 28–31+.

Shewell, John. "Focus on the Rock." *Science and Children* 31, no. 6 (March 1994): 28–29.

Woods, Robin K. "Simulating Glaciers." *Science Scope* 20, no. 2 (October 1996): 11–13.

Chapter 10

Coal Mining

In Coal Country

by Judith Hendershot
New York: Alfred A. Knopf, 1987

Summary

Life in Willow Grove revolved around the company coal mine. From the homes where the people lived to the stores where they shopped, the company exerted an influence on the miners. This story shows the everyday life of the miners and their families from the children's point of view. It is a way of life that has, for the most part, become obsolete. It is portrayed here in words and drawings about the time.

Science and Content Related Concepts

Natural resources, environment, coal and rock formations, life cycles, seasonal changes, mining, air and water pollution, life during the 1930s, self-sufficiency, shift work, transportation, household duties versus occupational duties, Pennsylvanian Era

Content Related Words

Hoot owl shift, company row, coal camp, tipple, gob piles, red dog, copper boiler, soot, paddy man, minerals, resources

Activities

1. Have children learn about the characteristics of coal using a "mystery box" and their sense of touch. Cut a hole, large enough for a child's hand, into the end of a shoe box (see fig. 10.1). Place a lump of coal inside and seal the shoe box. Do not tell children what is inside the box. Have them feel this mystery object and list adjectives and phrases that describe it, as well as guesses about the identity of the object. Repeat the activity using pieces of coal of various sizes, shapes, and textures. NOTE: Perhaps this activity is best done before beginning the unit (and before telling children that this unit is about coal).

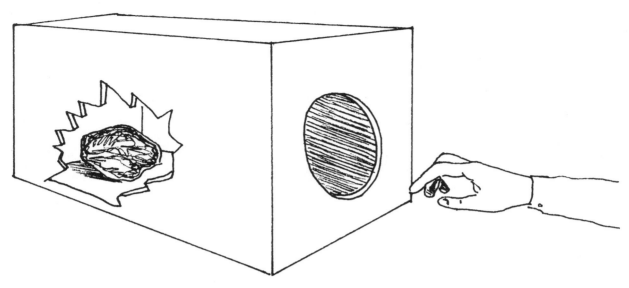

Fig. 10.1. Coal Mystery Box.

2. Is it possible to see air pollution? Have children try this experiment in a darkened room: Shine a flashlight against the wall and clap two chalk-filled erasers together near the flashlight. What do children see in the beam of light? Use water-filled spray bottles to simulate rain, and flap a piece of cardboard to simulate wind, to try to clear the air of pollution.

3. Show children the effects of coal pollution on rivers and streams: Cut the top off of a two-liter soda bottle and fill the bottom half with water. Have the children add several pieces of coal and mix the water and coal using a spoon. What happens? How might children clean the water? Filtering the water using coffee filters or paper towels is one possibility. Have children clean the water and compare it to tap water.

4. Have children make pollution "catchers" (see fig. 10.2): Attach a piece of waxed paper to a cardboard frame, and lightly coat the waxed paper with petroleum jelly. Place catchers in various locations throughout the community. Label each catcher with the location. After three days of exposure to the elements, have children collect the catchers and compare levels of air pollution.

5. Have children research modern mining and pollution-control methods and compare them to the methods portrayed in the story. What are the differences? What are the similarities?

6. Have children survey their parents and grandparents to learn whether any were involved or lived in a coal camp. Perhaps they remember a time when coal was burned to produce heat. Invite them to visit the class and share their "living history" stories.

7. Discuss the gender roles implied by the activities of the parents in the story. Have children compare and contrast these gender roles to the modern roles implied by their parents' activities. Have children perform a skit to show the differences.

8. Discuss shift work. Ask children what jobs today make use of shifts. Are uniforms worn for these jobs?

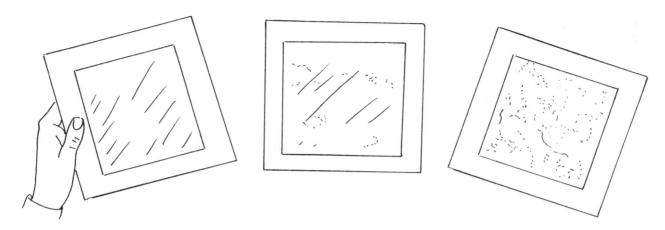

Fig. 10.2. Pollution Catchers.

9. Laundry boards can still be found in many hardware stores. Obtain one and have children try to wash some clothes.

10. Ask the class if anyone can explain the process of canning vegetables or other foods, such as pickles or jam. Have someone demonstrate and discuss the equipment used in this process. Have children compare canning to the more modern processes of preparing frozen, freeze-dried, and dehydrated food.

11. Make a chart comparing children of the time depicted in the book to modern-day children (e.g., household responsibilities, transportation to school and other places, games played).

12. Have children make a chart showing all of the places they go during the course of one week. How does their lifestyle compare to the isolation of living in a coal mining village?

13. Have children ask their parents and grandparents what games they played as children. Do any of them remember the rules for playing such games as King of the Mountain? Bring in the directions for various games and try them at recess.

14. Have children compose jump-rope rhymes about living in a coal mining village.

15. The children in the story ate Eskimo pies on payday. Have children brainstorm how the class might earn enough money to have the same special treat.

16. Self-sufficiency was the way of life during the time shown in the book. Have children locate examples of how family members depended on each other and used materials at hand instead of buying items (e.g., gathering nuts for Christmas baking).

17. Have children "mine for chips": Each child receives a chocolate chip cookie, a toothpick, and several one-inch sections of a drinking straw. The toothpick is used to remove (mine) chocolate chips from the cookie. Chocolate is put into the straw sections, and points are given for each section or partial section filled. Damage to the cookie (the environment) is assessed as a point penalty; the damage total is subtracted from the total earned by mining. The child with the highest score wins. NOTE: For an illustration of this activity, see page 81.

18. Have children grow a coal garden: Place lumps of coal or charcoal into a glass or plastic dish. Measure and mix together six tablespoons each of ammonia, water, salt, and laundry bluing. Add several drops of food coloring, if desired. Pour the mixture over the coal or charcoal and watch the garden grow. Small changes will occur on the first day, and there will be continual changes for the next several days. NOTE: An adult should handle the ammonia. Avoid breathing the fumes, and avoid contact with the skin. Mix the materials in a well-ventilated area.

19. Have children make pet "coal critters" from lumps of coal. Add craft eyes, pipe cleaners for legs, feathers, and other decorative materials as desired. Have children name each critter and write a story about its journey here from deep within the earth.

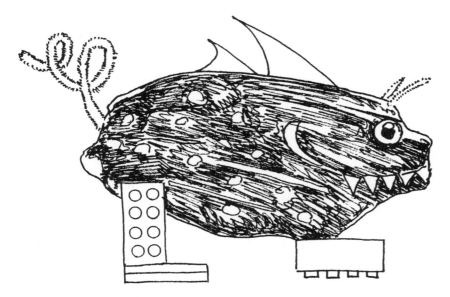

Fig. 10.3. Coal Critter.

20. Have children make a timeline to show when the plants from which coal was formed were alive. The existence of early humans and major groups of animals (e.g., dinosaurs, amphibians) should be noted on the timeline. Ask children why the period when coal deposits were formed is called the Pennsylvanian era.

21. Have children write a letter to the American Coal Foundation, inquiring about available materials:

> American Coal Foundation
> 1130 17th Street, NW
> Suite 220
> Washington, DC 20036
> (202) 466-8630
> www.ket.org/Trips/Coal/ACF.html

22. On a large map of the world, have children mark and label major deposits of coal. (An encyclopedia can be used to locate deposit areas.) Have children locate the site of the story (Knifes, Ohio) and trace the shipping route for the coal as it was moved by railroad from the camp and carried onto the Ohio River on barges.

23. Have children bring to class various model train cars (engines, flat cars, coal cars, etc.) from family collections.

24. Here are three story starters based on *In Coal Country*. Allow each child to select one of these topics and use it to develop a story about their own lives: "In the summer when it was hot, the kids . . ."; "In the autumn, the hills were ablaze with color . . ."; and "Christmas was the best time of the year. . . ."

25. Life in the mining village portrayed in the story was quite different than life today. Ask children if they would rather live during those days or today. In writing, have children explain the reasons for their choice.

26. Crossword—*In Coal Country*

CLUES

Across

1. Mother used this process to preserve food
3. Specific time when one worked at the mine (three words)
6. Pile of waste material (two words)
7. Wash boilers were made of this metal
8. He repaired the railroads (two words)
9. Streets were made of this material (two words)
10. Substances dug from the ground
13. They carried the coal to Ohio
18. Pa wore these to protect his feet (three words)

Down

1. Dug from the ground in the mines
2. Group of houses in a coal mining village (two words)
4. Device to wash and sort coal
5. Pa wore trousers made from this faded cloth
10. Underground area containing coal
11. Pa shelled these for Mother's Christmas cakes
12. Flowers for Mother's table
14. It signified the end of a shift or work time
15. Pail to carry a lunch
16. These animals worked in the mines
17. State near Pennsylvania and West Virginia

WORDS USED

bucket	hoot owl shift	red dog
canning	mine	steel-toed shoes
coal	minerals	tipple
company row	mules	trains
copper	nuts	violets
denim	Ohio	whistle
gob pile	paddy man	

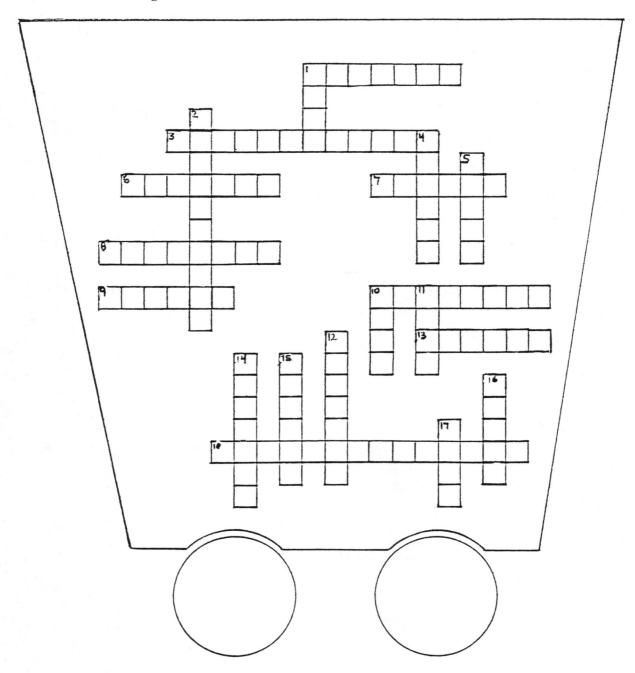

Fig. 10.4. Crossword—*In Coal Country.*

Related Books and References

Hendershot, Judith. *Up the Tracks to Grandma's*. New York: Alfred A. Knopf, 1993.

Langdon, Robert J. "Dig into Mining Activities." *Science Scope* 19, no. 1 (September 1995): 28–33.

Lynn, Loretta. *Coal Miners Daughter*. MCA Records 936.

McBiles, Larry. "From the Mine to My Home." *Science Scope* 17, no. 8 (May 1994): 28–29.

Shewell, John A. "Technology and 'Buried Sunshine.' " *Science Scope* 18, no. 5 (February 1995): 35–36.

Chapter 11

Earth Processes

On the Day You Were Born

by Debra Frasier
San Diego, CA: Harcourt Brace Jovanovich, 1991

Summary

Earth and all of its creatures, as well as the stars in all of the universe, were ready for the day you were born. The universe exists in harmony and provides a world for life's creatures.

Science and Content Related Concepts

Diversity, relationships in the world, rotation of Earth, revolution of Earth, phases of the Moon, water cycle, birth process, Beaufort Scale, heliography

Content Related Words

Gravity, tides, mantle, environment, ozone layer, migration, prominence

Activities

At the end of the story is a section titled "More About the World Around You." This section explores 11 areas of interest that amplify and explain relationships found on Earth. Activities for each of those areas are outlined here, in the first 11 activities.

1. Migrating Animals
    a. Children's task is to observe animals in motion. Have them do this by viewing video selections about animals, from either the library media center or from a rental source. How are the movements of various animals similar to the movements of human beings? How are the movements different? To test children's hypotheses, hold a "Pet Day"—have children bring their pets to class. Have children describe the movements of the animals using artwork, sculpture, dance, dramatization, pantomime, and writing.

    b. Animals migrate over great distances—distances that cannot be physically equaled by human beings without reliance on technology. Ask children why they think that animals migrate. Ask a library media specialist to help children find books or magazines about the migration of animals, such as birds, butterflies, salmon, and whales. Have children trace these migrations on a map of the world. NOTE: There are instances of migrations made by human beings, such as those for the purpose of finding employment or escaping winter weather in the northern states of the United States. Have children discuss human migrations.

2. Spinning Earth

    a. A sundial can help children visualize the rotation of Earth by implication. Early on a sunny day, drive a large spike into an open, grassy area. Drive a smaller stake into the grass at the end of the line created by the shadow of the large spike, about 15 feet from the spike (see fig. 11.1). Every hour, return to the sundial and drive another stake into the grass at the end of the shadow. If some children in the class live near the school, they may want to continue driving stakes until nightfall. What can children conclude about the movement of Earth? NOTE: A sundial can also be made by placing a large stake into a bucket of sand on the playground. The shadows cast can be drawn in the sand.

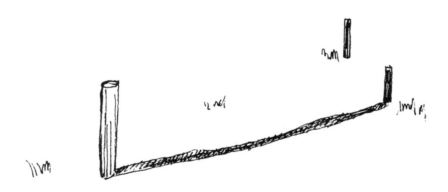

Fig. 11.1. Sundial.

    b. Because of the rotation of Earth, we experience a new day every 24 hours. Have children choose their favorite time of the day and write a story about how they enjoy that period of time. Have children share their stories with others in the class. They might categorize their stories (e.g., three children who enjoy recess best, two children who prefer soccer practices to other events, four children who spend their free time playing Nintendo). Make a bar graph to chart and compare the most popular activities in which children take part.

3. Pulling Gravity

    Gravity keeps us on Earth; otherwise we would float into the air. Have children imagine how life would be on an Earth without gravity. Have children pantomime the situation that would occur in each of the following circumstances:

    Riding a roller coaster

    Putting books on a shelf

    Putting dishes into a dishwasher

    Pouring juice into a glass

    Diving off a diving board

Shoveling dirt

Tossing a newspaper onto the porch

Playing basketball

Emptying dishwater down the drain

Playing dress up

Riding a bike

Floating down a river

Putting objects into your pocket

Climbing a tree

4. Flaming Sun
   a. The Sun emits radiant energy, which we experience in the forms of heat and light. To determine effects of heat from the Sun, have children build a reflecting device by lining a shoe box with aluminum foil. Place a small, flat dish of water into the shoe box; take the temperature of the water and record it. Tightly cover the top of the box with plastic wrap. Place the box in a sunny spot where it will not be disturbed. After about 30 minutes, have children measure the temperature of the water using a thermometer. Continue measuring the temperature of the water in the box every 30 minutes for two to three hours. How warm does the water become? How does heat from the Sun affect life on Earth? Can the Sun's heat be harnessed to produce energy? What would happen if this experiment was performed on a cloudy day? Have children try the experiment on a cloudy day to test their hypotheses.

   b. To show the importance of sunlight to life on Earth, have children try this experiment: Put one of two small, identical plants in full sunlight on a window sill. Put the other plant in a shoe box and put the lid on the box; place the box on the window beside the uncovered plant. The uncovered plant will receive light and heat from the Sun; the covered plant will only receive heat. Water the plants with equal amounts of water every three days. After five or six days, have children observe the leaves and stems of the plants. What has happened to the plant in the box? Which plant appears to be healthier? What can children conclude about the importance of sunlight to plants? Discuss how sunlight affects humans (e.g., sunny days often make people feel happier; dark, overcast days often make people feel sadder or a little depressed). Ask children how they feel when the weather changes.

5. Glowing Moon
   a. The Moon can be seen from Earth because it reflects light from the Sun. Have children simulate this reflective quality by using a small mirror. Hold the mirror so that the sunlight strikes it. Maneuver the mirror so that the reflection changes position. Communication using mirrors to reflect sunlight is called heliography. Have children devise a set of brief and long reflective "pulses," similar to the dots and dashes of Morse code, and send messages to each other across the playground. NOTE: Explain to children not look directly at the sun or at its reflection. It can damage their eyes.

   b. On a clear night, have children observe the Moon. They will notice that the Moon is not entirely white. There are shades of gray, which often suggest shapes, such as the "Man in the Moon," to the observer. Have children write down or draw their impressions of the surface of the Moon as seen by the naked eye. In class, have children share their impressions. Show the class a detailed drawing of the Moon (e.g., see *National Geographic Atlas of the World* by John B. Garver Jr. and others). What causes the appearance of a "Man in the Moon"? NOTE: If possible, have children extend their observation of the Moon by using binoculars.

6. Glittering Star
   a. On a clear night, have children find Polaris, also known as the North Star. It is in line with the stars in the Little Dipper constellation (see fig. 11.2). Have children position themselves so that they face the North Star. When walking towards the star, a person is moving in a northerly direction. What things in the immediate surroundings are to the north (e.g., neighbor's garage, swing set)? Have children face the North Star and then locate south, east, and west. NOTE: The position of the North Star as seen from Earth remains nearly constant because it is located along the axis around which Earth rotates. The North Star does not appear to move across the sky as most stars do, so it is useful for determining direction. Since ancient times, people have used the North Star as a means for orienting themselves.

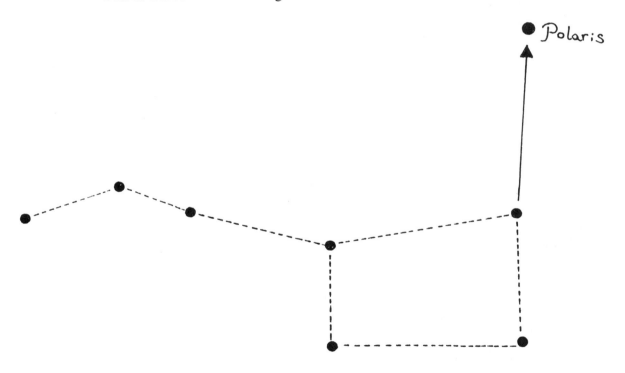

Fig. 11.2. Locating the North Star.

   b. Venus is the second planet from the Sun and is closest in size to the Earth. Because it can be easily seen at dusk and at sunrise, it is often mistaken as a star. However, its bright light is a reflection of the Sun's light. When Venus rises in the western sky at sunset, it is known as the Evening Star; when it rises in the eastern sky at sunrise, it is known as the Morning Star. Have children try to find these two "stars."

7. Rising Tide

   a. Have children observe the rising and falling of the tides by enjoying a video, such as *Let's Explore a Seashore*, published by the National Geographic Society. This video shows the tidal and intertidal zones of a beach along the coast of Maine and introduces the viewer to myriad sea creatures that live in these zones between the land and the open sea.

      National Geographic Society
      17th and M Street NW
      Washington, DC 20036
      (202) 857-7000
      www.nationalgeographic.com/main.html

   b. The creatures of the intertidal zone are illustrated in figure 11.3. The names of the creatures are given below. Divide the class into groups and assign each group several creatures to find. Have groups write the number of each creature on a master copy of figure 11.3. Gather related books, magazines, and posters from the library media center to assist children in their search. A useful resource is *Seashores: A Guide to Shells, Sea Plants, Shore Birds, and Other Natural Features of American Coasts* by Herbert Zim.

Match the names below with the animals and plants in figure 11.3. Place the number of each item in the proper square.

   1. Sea Squirt
   2. Jelly Fish
   3. Deadman's Finger Sponge
   4. Channel Whelk & Egg Case
   5. Brittle or Daisy Star
   6. Sea Anemone
   7. Crumb of Bread Sponge
   8. Flounder
   9. Sea Cucumber
   10. Rock Crab
   11. Kelp
   12. Sea Urchin
   13. Soft Shell Clam
   14. Sand Worm
   15. Hermit Crab
   16. Dog Whelk
   17. Blue Mussel
   18. Limpet

   19. Chiton
   20. Skate
   21. Lobster
   22. Periwinkle
   23. Deep Sea Scallop
   24. Amphipod
   25. Plankton
   26. Herring Gull
   27. Sand Dollar
   28. Skate Egg Case
   29. Moon Snail Collar
   30. Moon Snail Shell
   31. Starfish
   32. Irish Moss
   33. Rockweed
   34. Barnacle
   35. Horseshoe Crab

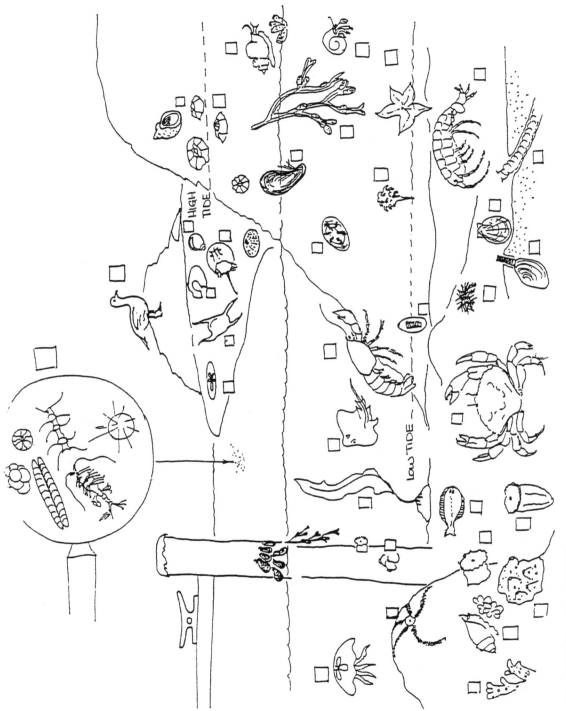

Fig. 11.3. The Intertidal Zone.

From *More Science Through Children's Literature.* © 1998 Butzow and Butzow. Teacher Ideas Press. (800) 237-6124.

8. Falling Rain

   a. Falling rain is part of the water cycle. For a hands-on experience with the water cycle, have children try playing the game Water-Cycle Water Journey: Assign each of nine children a number that corresponds to one step of the water cycle. Steps #1 and #10 are both the ocean, so one child should play both parts. Have children form a circle and kick a soccer ball from player to player in the order of the water cycle: #1 (ocean) kicks to #2 (evaporation/cloud); #2 kicks to #3 (rain); #3 kicks to #4 (mountain); #4 kicks to #5 (stream); #5 kicks to #6 (river); #6 kicks to #7 (estuary); #7 kicks to #8 (harbor); #8 kicks to #9 (bay); #9 kicks to #10 (ocean). Begin the cycle again. NOTE: For related activities, see Chapter 12, "The Sun and Its Effects" (in this book) or Chapter 21, "Water," in *Science Through Children's Literature*.

9. Growing Trees

   a. Much can be learned about trees by studying their leaves with a magnifying lens or microscope. Have children study various leaves. What is the shape? Is the edge smooth or rough? Look for the veins, which carry nourishment to the tree. Are there small holes on the surface of the leaf through which it takes in and lets out gasses? NOTE: Use leaves from both broad-leafed and needle-leafed trees. Gather leaves carefully so as not to harm the trees.

   b. Have children make leaf rubbings by placing a sheet of paper on top of a leaf and rubbing over the leaf with the edge of a crayon. Cut out the rubbings and paste them onto colored paper to make attractive wall hangings. NOTE: See also activity 2 in Chapter 6, "Life Cycle of Trees."

   c. Have children identify and map the trees in the schoolyard. With the help of the principal and the PTA, have children plant a tree in the schoolyard. Have them use a nursery catalog to help research and plan this endeavor. Should the tree be planted in a sunny or shady location? Will the location allow enough room for the tree to reach its full-grown size? What kind of tree should be planted? A fruit tree? A flowering tree? An evergreen? A broad-leafed tree? What is involved in caring for the tree? Does it need a specific type of soil? At what time of the year should the tree be planted? NOTE: Perhaps plant the tree in conjunction with an Arbor Day celebration on the last Friday of April or whenever it is set by the state government. Contact the National Arbor Day Foundation for information about this holiday. For a wide selection of trees, including seedlings that might be purchased for individual children, contact Musser Forests, Inc.; or, visit a local nursery.

      National Arbor Day Foundation
      100 Arbor Avenue
      Nebraska City, NE 68410
      (402) 474-5655
      www.arborday.org

      Musser Forests, Inc.
      P.O. Box 340
      Indiana, PA 15701-0340
      (412) 465-5685

d. Children know how old they are because their parents have told them their date of birth, and because they celebrate a birthday every year. Ask children how one can determine the age of a tree. Trees grow much more in the summer than in the winter. This produces rings in the cross section of the tree—one ring for each year of growth. Figure 11.4 shows the cross section of a Scotch pine that was used as a Christmas tree. The tree stood seven feet tall when it was cut in November 1996. Have children estimate its birth date.

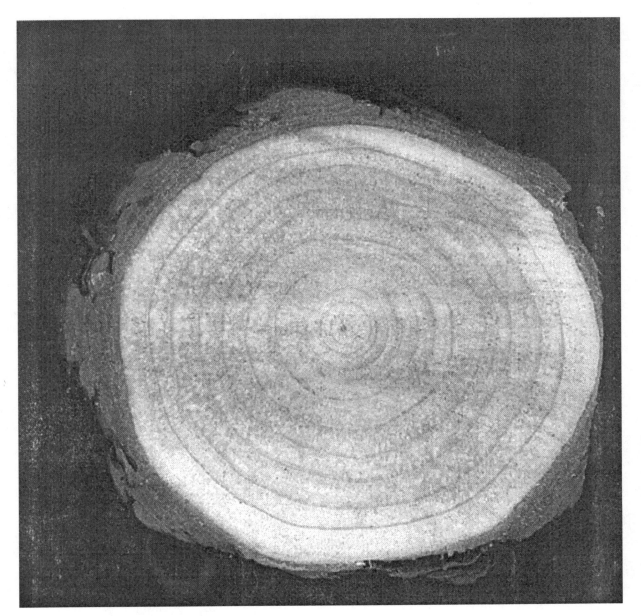

Fig. 11.4. Cross Section of a Scotch Pine.

10. Rushing Air

    a. When air is heated, it rises, and cold air from below takes its place. This movement of air is known as wind. The force of wind can range from a gentle breeze to a fierce hurricane. Have children research the highest wind speed clocked in your area. Is the wind ever so strong that it prevents children from doing what they want to do? Have children study the Beaufort scale, which equates wind speeds with common objects and activities.

    b. To see how air rises when heated, have children try this experiment: Remove the shade from an electric lamp. Turn on the lamp and let the bulb heat for two to three minutes. Clap two chalk-filled erasers together over the bulb and watch what happens. The tiny particles of chalk dust will rise above the bulb because they are floating in rising, warm air. NOTE: Caution children not to touch the bulb during or after the activity.

    c. Have children make a pollution "catcher": Fill a bucket halfway with water. Place the bucket in an open place where it is exposed to the air, but where it will not be disturbed. After one week, have children empty the bucket slowly into a coffee filter or into a finely woven piece of nylon stocking (see fig. 11.5). Spread the contents of the filter or nylon onto sheets of white paper and analyze them using a magnifying lens. What was filtered out of the water? How did the water "catch" these pollutants? What can children conclude about pollution? What are the sources of this pollution?

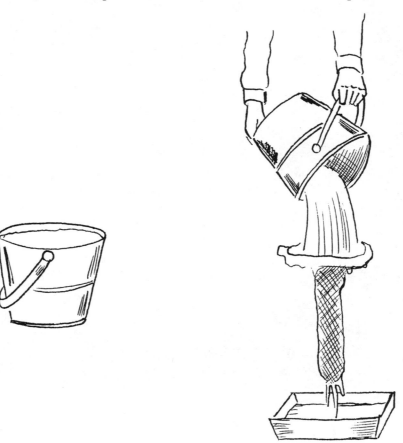

Fig. 11.5. Bucket Pollution Catcher.

    d.   Discuss with children the many ways that air affects our lives and our pastimes. NOTE: For additional activities related to air, see Chapter 20, "Kites, Wind, and Flight," and Chapter 21, "Airplanes and Flight."

11. Singing People

    a.   Select a theme and have children help produce an "Extravaganza Songfest" for parents or others in the school. Songs that can be presented as chorales work well. Perhaps produce an event in which every grade can contribute. The children will enjoy the sense of union as they become a special "Singing People." NOTE: A theme that works well for a celebration like this is diversity. Each grade might focus on a particular culture, including folk dances, ethnic foods, and selections of writing and poetry written by persons of that culture, as well as songs. As a finale, have all grades come together to sing "It's a Small World."

12. As a chance for children to share this unit with their families, have them interview family members about the day they (the children) were born. Children can obtain information by talking to relatives and friends who remember that day. Have children write down the events, including where they were born, who was there, why they were given their name, where they lived, their first toys, and so on. If a child was adopted by a family, have the child write about the day they came to live with that family.

13. Have children review and summarize what they have learned in this unit by playing Bingo. There are four categories of items: Earth, Sky, Water, and Animals. The caller calls out the name of an item or provides a clue to the identity of that item, which must then be guessed. Items matched on a card (see figs. 11.6–11.13) are covered with markers, such as pennies. A winning card has four markers in a row, across, down, or diagonal.

BINGO GAME WORD CLUES

Word   *Clue*

Earth

crust	the hard outer part of the Earth
rotation	revolving or turning
axis	the line about which an object rotates
equator	an imaginary line around the center of the Earth
gravity	force of the Earth's pull
population	the number of people
North Pole	the northern end of the Earth's axis
mantle	the inner layer of the Earth

Sky

planet	one of nine heavenly bodies revolving around the Sun
star	sun-like objects that produce their own light
Polaris	The North Star
constellation	a group of fixed stars that seem to form a picture
gas	the vapor state of matter
sun	body around which the planets revolve
moon	a body that revolves around a planet

Animals

butterfly	an insect with four broad wings
tern	a gull-like sea bird
salmon	a large edible ocean fish that spawns in fresh water
turtle	a hard-shelled land and sea reptile
eel	a snake-like fish
warbler	a song bird
whale	a large fish-like sea mammal
reindeer	a large northern deer

Water

condensation	liquid water that comes out of the vapor in the air
precipitation	water falling as rain, snow, etc.
tide	rise and fall of the ocean (often twice a day)
rain	water falling from the sky
vapor	the gaseous form of a liquid
evaporation	to change from liquid to gas or vapor
droplet	tiny amount of liquid

From *More Science Through Children's Literature.* © 1998 Butzow and Butzow. Teacher Ideas Press. (800) 237-6124.

Sky	Earth	Water	Animals
Polaris	axis	condensation	turtle
constellation	equator	precipitation	eel
gas	gravity	tide	warbler
sun	population	rain	whale

Fig. 11.6. Bingo Card.

Sky	Earth	Water	Animals
planet	crust	droplet	butterfly
star	rotation	vapor	tern
Polaris	axis	evaporation	salmon
constellation	equator	condensation	turtle

Fig. 11.7. Bingo Card.

From *More Science Through Children's Literature.* © 1998 Butzow and Butzow. Teacher Ideas Press. (800) 237-6124.

Sky	Earth	Water	Animals
moon	North Pole	vapor	butterfly
planet	crust	evaporation	tern
star	rotation	tide	salmon
Polaris	axis	precipitation	turtle

Fig. 11.8. Bingo Card.

Sky	Earth	Water	Animals
planet	gravity	rain	warbler
Polaris	population	droplet	whale
gas	mantle	vapor	reindeer
moon	North Pole	evaporation	butterfly

Fig. 11.9. Bingo Card.

Sky	Earth	Water	Animals
star	rotation	precipitation	warbler
Polaris	axis	tide	salmon
constellation	equator	rain	turtle
gas	gravity	droplet	eel

Fig. 11.10. Bingo Card.

Sky	Earth	Water	Animals
Polaris	population	tide	whale
gas	mantle	rain	reindeer
moon	North Pole	droplet	butterfly
planet	crust	vapor	tern

Fig. 11.11. Bingo Card.

From *More Science Through Children's Literature.* © 1998 Butzow and Butzow. Teacher Ideas Press. (800) 237-6124.

Sky	Earth	Water	Animals
constellation	equator	evaporation	turtle
moon	gravity	condensation	eel
Polaris	population	precipitation	warbler
gas	mantle	tide	whale

Fig. 11.12. Bingo Card.

Sky	Earth	Water	Animals
gas	axis	evaporation	whale
moon	North Pole	condensation	reindeer
planet	crust	precipitation	butterfly
star	rotation	tide	tern

Fig. 11.13. Bingo Card.

Related Books and References

Butzow, John, and Carol Butzow. *Science Through Children's Literature*. Englewood, CO: Teacher Ideas Press, 1989.

Cole, Joanna. *The Magic School Bus at the Water Works*. New York: Scholastic, 1986.

Connelly, Bernadine. *Follow the Drinking Gourd*. New York: Simon & Schuster, 1993.

Cronin, Jim. "Teaching Astronomy with Multicultural Mythology." *Science Scope* 20, no. 3 (November/December 1996): 15–17.

Foster, Gerald Wm. "Look to the Moon." *Science and Children* 34, no. 3 (November/December 1996): 30–33.

Garver, John B., Jr. et al. *National Geographic Atlas of the World*. 6th ed. Washington, DC: National Geographic Society, 1990.

Hutchinson, Elaine. "Rally Around Earth Month." *Science Scope* 16, no. 7 (April 1993): 29–31.

Lebofsky, Nancy R., and Larry A. Lebofsky. "Celestial Storytelling." *Science Scope* 30, no. 3 (November/December 1996): 18–21.

Let's Explore a Seashore. Washington, DC: National Geographic Society. Video 51607.

O'Dell, Marcy. "Turn the Tide on Trash." *Science and Children* 30, no. 4 (January 1993): 31–33.

Pederson, Jon, and Julie Thomas. "An Indoor Study of the Great Outdoors." *Science and Children* 29, no. 7 (April 1992): 18–19.

Savan, Beth. *Earthwatch: Earthcycles and Ecosystems*. Reading, MA: Addison-Wesley, 1992.

Williamson, Brad, and Orley Taylor. "Monarch Migration." *The Science Teacher* 63, no. 5 (May 1996): 26–29.

Zim, Herbert. *Seashores: A Guide to Shells, Sea Plants, Shore Birds, and Other Natural Features of American Coasts*. New York: Golden Press, 1955.

Chapter 12

The Sun and Its Effects

Sun Up

by Alvin Tresselt
New York: Lothrop, Lee & Shepard, 1949

Summary

The day was hot, without a cloud in the blue sky. Gradually, the dark clouds moved in and the jagged lightning forked through the sky. Then came the wind and the rain—beating down on everything until the Sun returned and a rainbow appeared in the sky.

Science and Content Related Concepts

Rotation of Earth, characteristics of summer, farm life, water cycle, electrical storms, dairy farming, milk production

Content Related Words

Sunrise, shadows, dewdrops, scorcher, thunder, lightning, rainbow, sunset

Activities

1. Before reading the story to the children, discuss the extremely hot days that they have experienced. How would they describe such high temperatures? How did they feel? What activities were they able to do? Unable to do? How did they "beat the heat?"

2. While reading aloud the story, discuss with children how the reader becomes aware, beforehand, that certain events will happen. This is because the reader is able to make predictions based on clues given in the text. Ask children what clues help them predict these events in the story:

Sunrise	Fair weather
Scorcher of a day	Rainbow
Storm	Sunset

   What predictions can children make about the weather for the day this story is being read?

3. In the story are names of several people, animals, events, and things. Have the children compile a list of these names. Their list should be similar to the list of words used for the word search (see activity 18).

4. From the list of words used for the word search (see activity 18), assign each child one or more words, so that all words are assigned. Have children draw a picture for each word they have been assigned. When the drawings are complete, have children sit in a large circle, and read aloud the story a second time. As each word is mentioned, the child with the picture of that thing should stand and show their picture to the rest of the class. Or, have children tape their pictures to the chalkboard as the words are mentioned, so that the pictures form a timeline of events in the story.

5. During their free time, children may want to dramatize the events of the story by playing with a set of plastic farmyard miniatures, building a model farm using Legos or Lincoln Logs, or by dressing in costumes and acting out the story.

6. The illustrator of *Sun Up*, Henri Sorensen, lives in Denmark. Sorensen's farm scene in *Sun Up* resembles the Danish countryside. In an atlas with landform maps, have children locate the country of Denmark. Does such a map help children understand the geography of the country? What are Denmark's major exports to the rest of the world? Have children sample some Danish cheese (e.g., *havarti*) from the delicatessen of a local grocery store.

7. In the library media center, have children locate the major regions for dairy farming in the United States, or find the areas of your state that are devoted to dairy farming. How does dairy farming contribute to the economy of this country? If possible, visit a dairy farm to see the daily operations of the farm.

8. Ask children what foods and beverages are considered to be dairy products. Sample some of them. NOTE: Dairy products usually include skim milk, 1% milk, 2% milk, whole milk, yogurt, sour cream, cream cheese, evaporated and condensed milk, ice cream, ice milk, frozen yogurt, butter, and cheese.

9. Dairy products are important sources of vitamins and minerals and provide energy for the human body. Ask children how this energy, which originates in the Sun, eventually becomes part of their bodies. Discuss figure 12.1, an energy flow chart, and have children pantomime the steps of this process or produce a short informational skit or advertisement about the importance of drinking milk.

10. To see the effects of high temperatures on the environment, have children try this experiment on a hot day when the air is still: Find two areas on the playground, one in the sunlight and one in the shade. Each area must remain sunny or shady for a couple of hours as the Earth rotates. In each area, place the following items: an aluminum pie tin containing a small amount of water, several pieces of cloth that have been wetted and wrung out, and wet sponges. Weight down these items so that they will not blow away. Have children check the items about every 30 minutes and observe what is happening to the water in each. In the classroom after the experiment, ask children to explain what happened to the items placed in the sunlight. Knowing that the Sun causes water to evaporate quickly, what can children conclude from this knowledge? NOTE: Because wind contributes to the evaporation of water, this experiment is best performed on a day when the air is still.

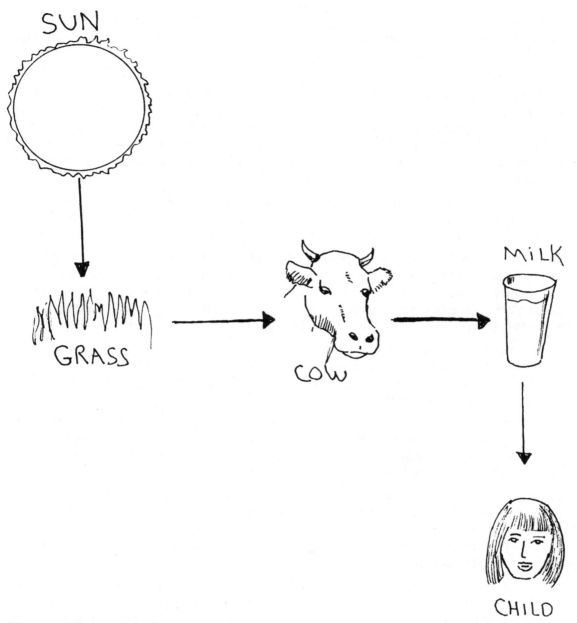

Fig. 12.1. Energy Flow Chart.

11. *Sun Up* is the story of a day on a farm, from early morning until evening. The change in light during the day is caused by the rotation of Earth. To simulate this effect, have one child play the role of the Sun by holding a flashlight and standing at the center of the room. Have the rest of the class form a circle around this child. Ask the child playing the Sun to choose a child in the circle to be Earth. This child should close their eyes and begin slowly rotating in place while the child playing the Sun shines the light on their head. What effect

does this rotation have on "Earth"? Is every part of the child's head illuminated by the flashlight at the same time? If the flashlight is shining on the child's face, this area of Earth would be experiencing daytime, while the rest of Earth, the back of the child's head, would be experiencing nighttime. When there is daylight in the United States, what countries are in darkness? How long does it take for Earth to complete one rotation? Allow each child a chance to play Earth. NOTE: To help children better visualize the rotation of Earth, use a flashlight and a plastic beach ball imprinted as a globe. Such globes are available from:

National Geographic Society
World Magazine
P.O. Box 2330
Washington, DC 20013
(202) 857-7000
www.nationalgeographic.com/main.html

12. Have children discuss how a typical day in their life is similar to or different from the day of the people in *Sun Up*. Have children make a timeline of their day, from the time they wake up until the time they go to bed. Is their day more affected by the rising and setting of the Sun or by the time? How is their life different when it is daylight savings time? How does their life change when standard time is reestablished? When does the day seem to be longest? Shortest? When does time seem to pass quickly? Slowly? Have children write an essay about time and how it affects their lives.

13. The Sun is an important part of the water cycle. Water from rivers, streams, lakes, and oceans evaporates into the air and forms clouds in the sky (see fig. 12.2). The water in the clouds condense into droplets, which fall to the earth as rain, snow, or hail. To simulate the water cycle, have children add one to two inches of warm water to a large, clear glass jar. Tightly place the lid on the jar, and set the jar in the sunlight. Eventually, droplets of water will appear on the inside of the jar and on the inside of the lid. This moisture falls to the bottom of the jar, or rolls down the sides of the jar. This water will eventually evaporate again as part of the continuous water cycle.

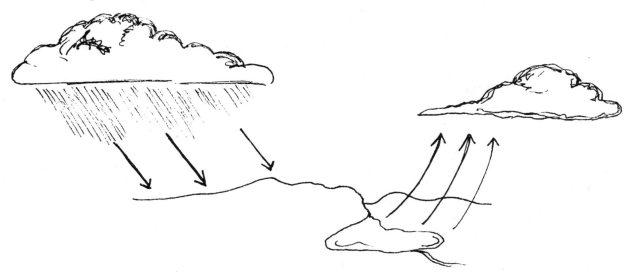

Fig. 12.2. Water Cycle.

14. The Sun affects our lives in many ways. Some effects can be harmful (e.g., looking at the Sun without eye protection can damage the eyes; working too hard in the heat from the Sun can result in heatstroke). For children, it is especially important to know the effects of the Sun's rays on the skin. Have the school nurse, a teacher, or a parent discuss the need for protecting the skin from the Sun's rays. What can happen to the skin if it is exposed to the Sun's rays over a prolonged period of time? What is the meaning of the numbering system that appears on sunscreen or sunblock? Why do people often expose themselves to the Sun's rays on a regular basis? What harmful effects should people be aware of when tanning? Do the Sun's rays affect the body in beneficial ways?

15. Cows play an important role in *Sun Up*. Using the Internet or materials in the library media center, have children locate information about and pictures of various breeds of cows. Have children do a keyword search on the Internet using *breeds of cattle*, which will produce information about farmers who raise Holstein (see fig. 12.3), Guernsey, Jersey, Brown Swiss, and Ayrshire cows, among other breeds. What are the distinguishing characteristics of these breeds (e.g., color, size, horns)? Does milk production vary from one breed to another? What are the positive and negative attributes of each breed? NOTE: Ask children if they have seen cows used in advertising, such as for an ice cream company or a computer business. Have children create an advertisement for something they like using a particular breed of cow.

Fig. 12.3. Holstein Cow.

16. Listening to music can help children visualize a scene in their mind. Ferde Grofe's *The Grand Canyon Suite* has movements called "Sunrise" and "The Storm." Ask children how these movements relate to the story *Sun Up*. What do they visualize when listening to these movements? Why? Have children draw pictures as they listen to these movements.

17. After the storm in *Sun Up*, a rainbow appears. Have children make a rainbow using these methods:

   a. Make a rainbow appear on a wall by passing a beam of light through a prism. NOTE: Prisms can be purchased at a science supply house, such as Edmonds Scientific.

b. Place a mirror in a clear bowl filled with water; adjust the mirror so that it rests at a 30-degree angle to the surface of the water. Darken the room and direct the beam of the flashlight at the mirror. A rainbow will appear on the ceiling.

c. Shine a focused beam of light through a large, clear container filled with water. (The beam of light from a slide projector is sufficiently focused to produce a rainbow.)

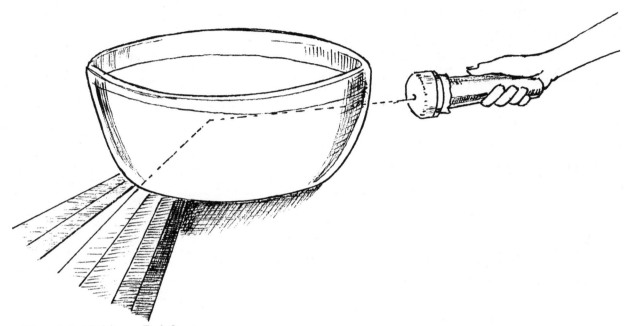

Fig. 12.4. Making a Rainbow.

Discuss the colors of a rainbow and how rainbows occur in nature. Have children draw pictures that contain rainbows.

18. Word Search—*Sun Up*

   Words from the story *Sun Up* are hidden in this word search—horizontally and vertically, forwards and backwards. First, match the words to the clues.

CLUES

a. It accompanied thunder

b. It announced that morning had begun

c. He was the father's assistant

d. Young man who went fishing

e. Bright yellow flower

f. It spun its web in the barn

g. Sudden rushes of rain, sometimes with thunder and lightning

h. It tied bundle of food for cows (two words)

i. Place where the animals drank

j. They swam in the pond

k. Place where the animals slept

l. Small, chirping insect

m. It could be seen in the sky

n. Small rodent

o. It flapped its wings in trying to fly

p. Kind of tree

q. Swiftly flowing water

r. Machine that helped the farmer plant and harvest

s. Man who owned the farm

t. Dark one may indicate a storm

u. Place where eggs were gathered

v. They were milked each day

w. Family's pet

WORDS USED

barn	farmer	rooster
boy	fish	spider
catbird	hay baler	storms
chicken	helper	stream
cloud	henhouse	sunflower
cows	lightning	sycamore
cricket	mouse	tractor
dog	pond	

```
S  U  N  F  L  O  W  E  R  B  O  Y  S
C  A  X  R  E  L  A  B  Y  A  H  W  M
R  Y  T  A  M  O  B  P  H  R  P  R  B
I  Q  R  C  H  I  C  K  E  N  R  T  X
C  S  A  T  A  F  L  B  N  C  O  W  S
K  Y  C  O  D  O  G  H  S  I  F  D
E  C  T  I  C  F  U  P  O  N  D  A  Z
T  A  O  M  A  C  D  K  U  C  E  R  V
A  M  R  S  T  O  R  M  S  L  R  M  Z
R  O  E  P  B  W  P  O  E  O  D  E  T
B  R  Q  I  I  G  E  U  L  U  H  R  V
S  E  F  D  R  O  H  S  M  D  C  G  S
F  T  B  E  D  P  H  E  L  P  E  R  L
C  A  H  R  O  O  S  T  E  R  I  K  I
L  I  G  H  T  N  I  N  G  A  J  B  M
D  N  E  H  E  D  F  O  H  S  T  V  T
S  T  R  E  A  M  X  Z  B  T  S  C  T
```

Fig. 12.5. Word Search—*Sun Up*.

Related Books and References

Allen, Thomas B. *On Grandaddy's Farm*. New York: Alfred A. Knopf, 1989.

Beethoven, Ludwig. *Symphony No. 6* (Pastoral). Cleveland Orchestra. George Szell.

Goh, Ngoh-Khang, Yoke-Kum Wan, and Lian-Sai Chia. "Simply Photosynthesis." *Science and Children* 31, no. 1 (September 1993): 32–34.

Grofe, Ferde. *The Grand Canyon Suite*. New York Philharmonic Orchestra. Leonard Bernstein.

McDuffie, Thomas E., and Bruce G. Smith. "Has Anyone Seen the 'I' in ROY G BIV?" *Science Scope* 18, no. 7 (April 1995): 30–33.

Chapter 13

Thunderstorms

Thunder Cake

by Patricia Polacco
New York: Philomel Books, 1990

Summary

When a little girl hides under the bed because of the thunder from an oncoming storm, her grandmother knows a sure cure for her fears. Making a thunder cake, complete with a secret ingredient, helps prove to the little girl that thunder has no power to harm anyone during a storm, and that she has actually been very brave.

Science and Content Related Concepts

Sound, storms, clouds, fear, baking, folk wisdom

Content Related Words

Thunder, bolt of lightning, electricity, sultry, horizon, air pressure, cold front, warm front, stationary front, trellis, babushka, samovar

Activities

1. *Thunder Cake* is the story of a grandmother who was born in Russia, but is now living in the state of Michigan. Using a globe, have children locate Russia and Michigan. Have them use the scale on the globe to find the distance between the grandmother's two homes.

2. Have children look up Michigan in the encyclopedia. Research the size of the state (see fig. 13.1), its landforms and lakes, its industries and agriculture, and its cities. Children will probably be interested in learning about Detroit and Battle Creek.

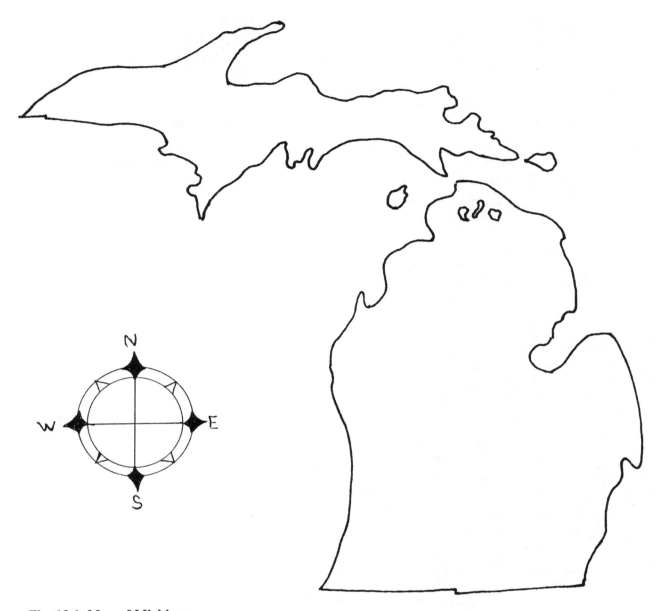

Fig. 13.1. Map of Michigan.

3. If possible, read this story to children on a hot day when a thunderstorm seems imminent. Should a storm ensue, have children use the grandmother's formula to approximate how far away the storm is: Each time the lightning flashed, she would count the number of seconds that elapsed before the thunderclap. For example, if 10 seconds elapse between the lightning flash and the thunderclap, the storm is 10 miles away. Have children look at a map of your county or metropolitan area. If a storm is 10 miles away, which town would the storm be closest to? If it is 20 miles away, where would the storm be?

4. Ask children to identify characteristics of the weather that immediately precedes a summer thunderstorm. How is this weather different from the weather that precedes a snowstorm, a tropical storm, or an autumn rainfall? Have children look at a weather map in the newspaper and notice the frontal systems that are indicated. What type of weather follows each of the fronts? Can children predict the weather for the next day by studying the frontal systems and understanding the changes in air pressure?

5. What is lightning? What is thunder? Ask children to share the stories they believed when they were younger about the origin and purpose of these two weather conditions. In the library media center, have children research the legends and folktales that people told to account for these events.

6. It is possible to create a tiny clap of thunder and a spark of electricity. Have children try these experiments:

   a. Inflate a paper lunch bag, hold the top closed with one hand, and break the bag by striking it with the palm of the other hand. This results in a rush of air, or thunder. In reality, the rush of air known as thunder is caused by the electrical discharge of lightning.

   b. Rub a plastic comb or ruler briskly with a piece of wool or fur. Touch the comb or ruler to a doorknob to produce a spark. These sparks are harmless, unlike a bolt of lightning, which can injure or kill. By what name do we call a spark produced in this way? Are there other ways to make a spark?

7. Try the experiment in activity 6b using a balloon instead of a comb or ruler. Have children touch the balloon to their arm. What happens? How is this related to lightning?

8. Have children try this experiment (see fig. 13.2), which is best performed on a day with low humidity: Tie a 12-inch thread onto a small Styrofoam ball. Rub the ball with wool or fur. Darken the room and let the ball hang loosely. Have a child move their finger towards the ball. What happens? Does the child feel anything? Is a sound produced? How can children explain this phenomenon? How is this related to *Thunder Cake*?

9. Clouds are an important component in the study of weather. Have a library media specialist help children locate a book about weather. Have children research the various types of clouds. What does each type indicate about the weather? What type of clouds are most often related to thunderstorms? What clouds are known as thunderheads? Ask a library media specialist to find newspaper or magazine articles about severe thunderstorms that have caused damage in your area. Based on these articles, have children determine how long a typical thunderstorm lasts. What changes in weather or precipitation often accompany a thunderstorm?

10. Have children draw pictures of the various types of clouds, including an illustration of the weather that typically accompanies each type.

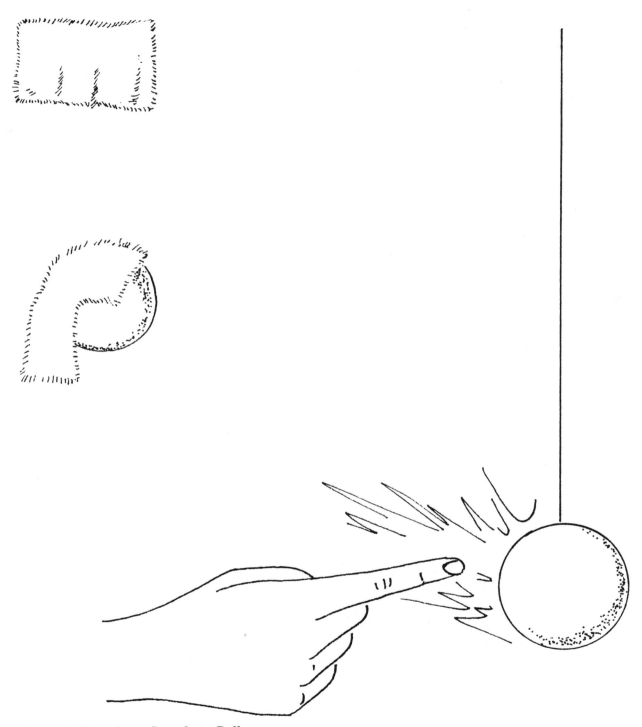

Fig. 13.2. Charging a Styrofoam Ball.

11. Is it possible to outrun a thunderstorm? Clock how fast (in seconds) children can run 20 yards. Using the chart below, determine their speed in miles per hour. Assuming that a storm moves at a speed of 20 miles per hour, how does each child's speed compare to that of a moving storm? Can anyone in the class run that fast? Ask a library media specialist to help children research animals that could possibly outrun a storm.

Time (Seconds)	Miles/Hour
1	40.9
2	20.5
Thunderstorm speed (20 m.p.h.)	
3	13.6
4	10.2
5	8.2
6	6.8
7	5.8
8	5.1
9	4.5
10	4.1
11	3.7
12	3.4
13	3.1
14	2.9
15	2.7
16	2.6
17	2.4
18	2.3
19	2.2
20	2.0

NOTE: For young children, it is probably best to give the numbers for miles/hour in round figures.

12. During a thunderstorm, it is best to take shelter from lightning in a house or in a car, or crouch on the ground. Ask children to identify things that they should avoid doing (e.g., standing under a tree). Have children make large posters to convey their ideas to others at school. To help children learn about being prepared for a storm, gather information about this topic from a local American Red Cross chapter. Ask for the pamphlet "Thunderstorms."

13. During a thunderstorm, it is not uncommon for lightning to cause an outage of electrical power. Ask children what they can do to be prepared for a loss of electricity. What precautions should they take to make this inconvenience less of a problem? It is important to plan ahead for a power outage, so that the needs of every family member can be met. Does the school have a contingency plan for power outages when children are in school? What if electricity will be out for an extended period of time?

14. Fear is a major theme in *Thunder Cake*. Have children discuss the feelings they have when they are afraid. Does their heart beat faster? Do they have a dry mouth? Do they feel cold

and clammy? Why do people often want to hide when they are afraid? Where would children go to feel safe during a threatening situation, such as a thunderstorm?

15. Have children each write two journal entries, one about a time when they were afraid, and one about a time when they thought they would be afraid, but were instead very brave.

16. "Whistle a Happy Tune," from the Broadway musical *The King and I*, and "My Favorite Things," from another Broadway musical *The Sound of Music*, were composed by Richard Rodgers and Oscar Hammerstein. These songs are sung to children who are afraid. Have children learn to sing these songs and discuss the emotions they feel when singing them. If possible, show the segments from the movies (of the same names) that contain these songs. Of what are the children in these movies afraid? Why do they feel better after singing?

17. As a class project, make the grandmother's thunder cake, or ask a child to make it at home and bring it to class for a snack time. Can children taste the secret ingredient? How does this cake compare to other cakes they have eaten?

18. Have children bring to class recipes for cakes and make a "Classroom Cake Cookbook" to be given as a present to parents, relatives, and special friends.

19. Drinking tea with thunder cake was important to the grandmother. Ask children what kinds of teas they have at home. What other kinds of teas can they name? Ask a library media specialist to help children research the importance of teas in other cultures (e.g., Japanese tea ceremonies). How does the grandmother's samovar compare to modern teapots?

20. Share with children the following expressions for describing weather:

    It's good weather for ducks.

    Rain before seven, clear before eleven.

    It's raining cats and dogs.

    It's raining buckets.

    When it rains, it pours.

    Every cloud has a silver lining.

    A sunshiny shower won't last an hour.

    Red sky in the morning, sailors take warning; red sky at night, sailors delight.

    Have children write sayings to describe other forms of weather.

21. Storms are an engaging source of visual imagery. Have children think of adjectives and short, imaginative phrases to describe the various forms and elements of weather (e.g., hailstorms, "partly cloudy" weather). Children may want to depict their ideas in the form of a drawing.

22. Have children read other books by Patricia Polacco, such as *Rechenka's Eggs*. What similarities do they see between the books? What do they learn about the grandmother?

23. If possible, have someone in the community teach children a few words of Russian. Besides "grandmother," what else does the word *babushka* mean? What is the purpose of a samovar?

24. Word Ladder—*Thunder Cake*

First, match the "Words Used" to the clues. Write the words in the puzzle blanks, which are formed around the words *thunder cake*.

CLUES

1. Secret ingredient in thunder cake

2. It accompanies thunder

3. Another name for "grandmother"

4. Place where animals are kept

5. Summer weather disturbances

6. Red fruit

7. Country where the grandmother was born

8. State by the Great Lakes

9. Sound of thunder

10. Place where the granddaughter gathered eggs

11. Place where the granddaughter hid—under the _____

WORDS USED

babushka
barn
bed
kaboom

lightning
Michigan
Nellie Peck Hen
Russia

strawberries
thunderstorms
tomato

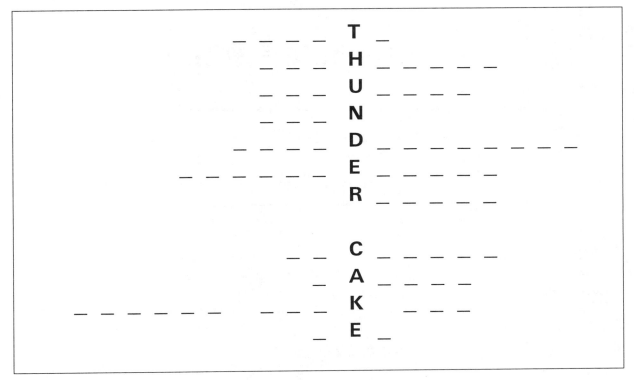

Fig. 13.3. Word Ladder—*Thunder Cake*.

From *More Science Through Children's Literature*. © 1998 Butzow and Butzow. Teacher Ideas Press. (800) 237-6124.

Related Books and References

Beethoven, Ludwig. *Symphony No. 6* (Pastoral). Cleveland Orchestra. George Szell.

Ostland, Karen L., and Michael A. DiSpezio. "Static Electricity, Dynamically Explored." *Science Scope* 19, no. 5 (February 1996): 12–13.

Polacco, Patricia. *Rechencka's Eggs*. New York: Philomel, 1988.

Rodgers, Richard, and Oscar Hammerstein. *The King and I*. Broadway cast recording. Prod. by the John F. Kennedy Center for the Performing Arts.

Rodgers, Richard, and Oscar Hammerstein. *The Sound of Music*. Movie soundtrack.

Chapter 14

Weather and Climate

Cloudy with a Chance of Meatballs

by Judi Barrett
New York: Atheneum, 1978

Summary

People in Chewandswallow never had to worry about buying or cooking food. It poured down from the sky. Good things never last, though, and the "rain" became too much. Reluctantly, the citizens had to move to a new town and leave behind their Chewandswallow.

Science and Content Related Concepts

Influence of weather, weather prediction, relationship of wind and weather, weather disasters, weather "cleanup," weather and habitation

Content Related Words

Wind, rain, snow, sleet, hail, showers, drifts, drizzle, gust, downpour, storm, hurricane, tornado, predict, meteorologist

Activities

1. Each day during morning activities, have one designated child present a local or state weather forecast for the day. The report should include the high and low temperatures, precipitation, humidity, wind speed and direction, and barometric pressure. Information can be obtained early each morning from radio, television, or the National Oceanographic and Atmospheric Administration (NOAA). Children can access NOAA information on the Internet at http://www.nnic.noaa.gov.

2. Another way to gather information for the morning forecast in activity 1 is to use newspapers. Have children work in small groups, each with a newspaper, to determine the weather predictions. They should look for photographs, articles, and advertisements that are used to announce weather predictions. Explain to children how to read weather maps as a means of predicting the weather. NOTE: A classroom subscription to a local newspaper is invaluable during this unit.

3. Assign individuals or small groups to the task of checking the weather periodically during the day to verify if the morning predictions were correct. Have children keep a log (see fig. 14.1) that includes high and low temperatures, precipitation, humidity, wind speed and direction, and barometric pressure. At the end of each week, have children record the week's highest and lowest temperatures, most precipitation, windiest day, and the highest and lowest barometric pressures.

4. Children may want to watch a local weather show or a cable weather channel before they present weather forecasts to the class, or before making weather videos. Discuss the presentations of a cable weather channel for content and style. Discuss how televised weather reports are presented. Is each report a forecast for one day's weather, or does each report involve forecasts for several days? What use is made of weather maps? How are visual displays used? Is supplementary weather information (e.g., a smog index) provided?

   After children have become comfortable with local weather forecasting, expand the daily forecast from having a single weather person to presenting a "national morning weather show," with an anchor person and a staff of meteorologists. Videotape the presentations over several days until everyone has had a chance to participate. Edit the tape to make a polished weather video for visitors to view.

5. Have children select various cities and track their weather for one week. Children should select areas that are geographically different from their locale (e.g., if they live in Pennsylvania, they should track the weather of a city in Florida or Washington). NOTE: This activity provides an excellent opportunity for doing jigsaw puzzles of the United States, as well as for making use of maps of the 50 states (see fig. 14.2).

6. Many television stations have a scholastic program in which a meteorologist meets the students at a school assembly or in a classroom. Have children research the availability of such a program in your area.

7. Invite a member of the local municipal department of public works to visit the class and discuss the functions of the department and the cost of "cleaning up" the weather. Have children ask questions, such as: How many workers does the department employ? How many vehicles, and of what types, are used? How long does it take to clean up a major snowstorm? What is the cost of road maintenance (i.e., snow removal, sanding, leaf removal, repairs to washouts and potholes). Ultimately, who pays for road maintenance? What happens during a severe winter when supplies are exhausted earlier than planned?

8. Have children talk with parents, grandparents, and other members of the community about weather disasters they have experienced. Have children prepare a community weather journal using written stories, photographs, and news articles. For example, community members may remember the 1972 hurricane Agnes, the great Midwest flood of 1993, or the Northeast blizzard of 1996. Many such catastrophes have been so noteworthy that communities have memorialized them (e.g., two museums are dedicated to the great Johnstown, PA, flood of 1889).

	Monday	Tuesday	Wednesday	Thursday	Friday
High Temperature					
Low Temperature					
Precipitation					
Humidity					
Wind Speed					
Wind Direction					
Barometric Pressure					

Fig. 14.1. Weather Log.

From *More Science Through Children's Literature*. © 1998 Butzow and Butzow. Teacher Ideas Press. (800) 237-6124.

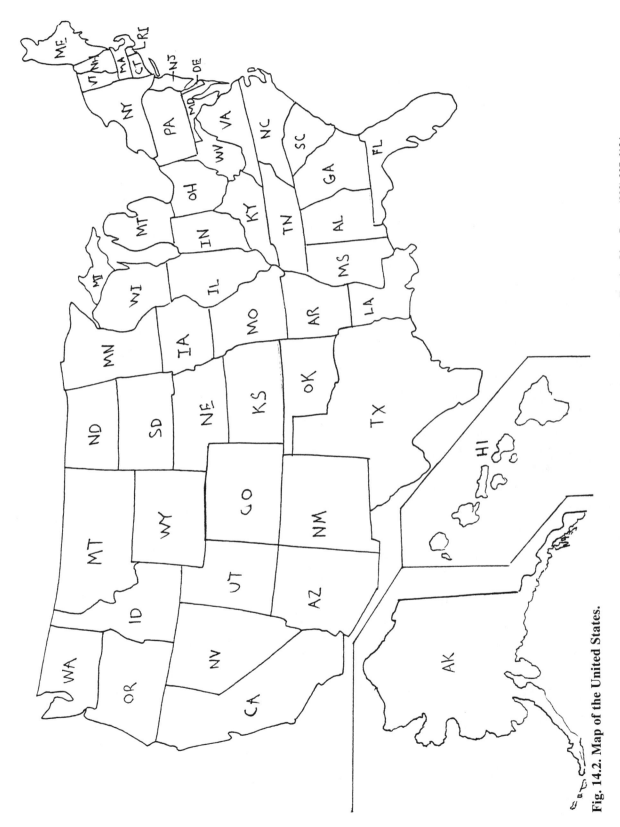

Fig. 14.2. Map of the United States.

9. Accuweather is a private weather forecasting service that provides information and materials related to the study of weather. To inquire about a membership, have children contact Accuweather on the Internet at http://www. accwx.com or by mail:

> Accuweather
> 619 West College Avenue
> State College, PA 16801
> (814) 237-0309

10. Rising barometric pressure is usually indicative of clearing weather. Falling barometric pressure is usually indicative of an approaching storm. Have children study the barometric pressure in your area for a few days. What conditions do they observe when the barometric pressure is high? When it is low? When it is changing rapidly? When it is changing slowly?

11. Have children make a door-sized thermometer from construction paper. Select several temperatures that are typical for your locale. Have children make and paste beside the thermometer pictures of children who are wearing appropriate clothing for those temperatures (see fig. 14.3). Have children make a second door thermometer, this one for an area that has a different climate than your locale (e.g., if you live in Virginia, try states such as Arizona or Minnesota).

12. Ask children if the school has storm days, when school is canceled because of severe weather. How many? What if all of the storm days for one year have been used and still another weather problem develops? Who decides if school should be canceled? What criteria do these people use when making this decision? How can someone determine whether school has been canceled? Have children write the answers to these questions in the form of a news release to share with other classes.

13. Have children read other books about children and weather (e.g., *Time of Wonder* by Robert McCloskey, *Gilberto and the Wind* by Marie Hall Ets, *Katy and the Big Snow* by Virginia Lee Burton, and *The Snowy Day* by Ezra Jack Keats). Have children try writing weather-related stories.

14. Have children illustrate the following expressions about weather:

> It's always fair weather.
>
> Every cloud has a silver lining.
>
> It's raining cats and dogs.
>
> It's good weather for ducks.
>
> Red sky in the morning, sailors take warning; red skies at night, sailors delight.
>
> Have children ask their parents or other teachers for more weather-related expressions.

15. Have children pretend that they are citizens of Chewandswallow. They have had to move to another town, where the food does not fall from the sky. Have children write down their feelings about living in the new town, now that food does not fall from the sky and they must go to the grocery store to buy food.

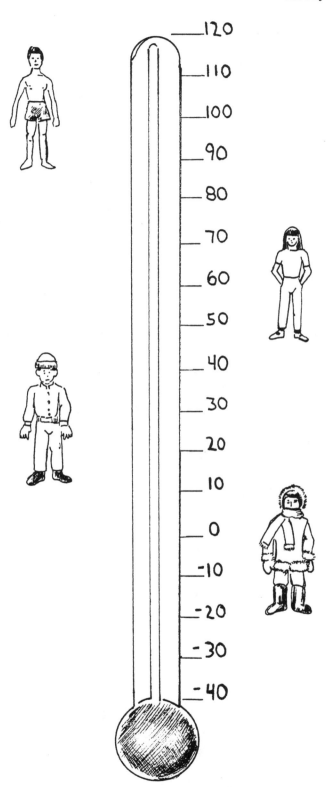

Fig. 14.3. Activity Thermometer.

16. Word Scramble—Weather

Words related to weather are given below in scrambled form. Use the accompanying clues to unscramble the words. The order of the clues does not necessarily follow the order in which the scrambled words are listed.

stug	tesle	zidelzr
swon	woresh	nowpurdo
laih	chianerur	ridft
dotanro	niar	dreunth
diwn		

CLUES

a. Sudden push of wind

b. Pile of snow, usually blown into place

c. Funnel-shaped storm

d. Movement of air, ranging from a breeze to a hurricane

e. Water droplets that fall to the earth

f. Balls of ice accompanying rainfalls or snowstorms

g. To rain gently in fine, mistlike drops

h. Crystals of ice that fall to the earth

i. Sudden, heavy rainfall

j. Freezing rain

k. Storm bearing significant rainfall and winds

l. Brief occurrence of rain, generally light in nature

m. Loud noise following lightning

WORDS USED

downpour	hurricane	snow
drift	rain	thunder
drizzle	shower	tornado
gust	sleet	wind
hail		

Related Books and References

Burton, Virginia Lee. *Katy and the Big Snow*. Boston: Houghton Mifflin, 1943.

Domel, Rue. "You Can Teach About Acid Rain." *Science and Children* 31, no. 2 (October 1993): 25–28.

Emery, Dave. "A Constructivist Cloud Lab." *Science Scope* 20, no. 2 (October 1996): 18–19.

Ets, Marie Hall. *Gilberto and the Wind*. New York: Viking, 1963.

Jones, M. Gail, and Glenda Carter. "Weather Folklore: Fact or Fiction." *Science and Children* 33, no. 1 (September 1995): 19–20.

Keats, Ezra Jack. *The Snowy Day*. New York: Viking, 1963.

McCloskey, Robert. *Time of Wonder*. New York: Viking, 1957.

Pinkham, Chester K., and Kristin Burrows Barrett. "Measuring Relative Humidity." *Science and Children* 30, no. 1 (September 1992): 23–27.

Chapter 15

Space Science

My Place in Space

by Robin Hirst and Sally Hirst
New York: Orchard, 1988

Summary

When the bus driver asked Henry where he lived, little did he realize that Henry would list all of his terrestrial and celestial homes. It was truly a trip to outer space and back.

Science and Content Related Concepts

Outer space, hierarchical classification of space, addresses

Content Related Words

Hemisphere, Earth, the solar system, solar neighborhood, Orion Arm, Milky Way, Virgo Supercluster, universe

Activities

1. Many ancient cultures had myths and stories to describe their concepts of the universe (e.g., some ancients thought that the universe was carried on the back of a turtle). Other stories explained the existence of the celestial bodies. Have a library media specialist help children find myths and stories about the universe.

2. Naked-eye astronomy refers to observations that can be made without the use of telescopes. Have children observe the sky on a clear night to see the various colors that appear. They should see celestial objects or bodies that range in color from red to yellow to bluish white. Have children make a color diagram of what they see using paper and crayons or colored chalk. NOTE: Each month, the stars that can be seen by the naked eye are shown in a star chart in the magazine *Science and Children*.

3. Have children estimate the number of stars that can be seen by the naked eye from their location on Earth: At arm's length, hold a sheet of clear acetate (such as transparency paper) up to the sky and, using a magic marker, mark each star that is seen (see fig. 15.1). Approximate how much of the visible sky was covered by the sheet, as a fraction with 1 in the numerator ($\frac{1}{4}$, $\frac{1}{2}$, etc.). To estimate the number of stars, multiply the number of stars

on the sheet by the denominator of coverage (e.g., if 30 stars are marked and the sheet covered ¼ of the sky, there are an estimated 120 stars in the sky). NOTE: For young children, an adult should do this activity and then explain it to children. Remind children that the estimate is not for the total number of stars in the sky, but for the number of stars visible to the naked eye as viewed from their location on Earth.

Fig. 15.1. Estimating the Number of Stars.

4. Have children use a children's astronomy book as a reference to help them learn about the characteristics of the various celestial objects and bodies. Have them make a diagram of the solar system using black paper and crayons or colored chalk.

5. Have children write poetry about celestial objects or bodies, such as planets, moons, stars, comets, asteroids, galaxies, or nebulae. Have children use "form poetry" to help them express their thoughts about a particular celestial object or body. Try the following sample form:

> Line 1—Name of the object
>
> Line 2—Two adjectives to describe the object
>
> Line 3—Three participles to describe the object
>
> Line 4—Short, descriptive phrase
>
> Line 5—Synonym for the object, or repeat the name of the object

NOTE: For the purposes of this activity, a participle is a word ending in *-ed* or *-ing* that functions as an adjective.

Example

> Moon
> Round, rocklike
> Waxing, waning, orbiting
> Astronauts have visited
> Satellite

6. Have children "adopt" a planet or celestial body to study. They should make a drawing of the planet or body and write a description (perhaps the poem from activity 5). Remind children that the most up-to-date information about space is often found on the Internet (see activity 20) or in astronomy magazines. So many discoveries are being made about space that textbooks become dated almost as soon as they are published. Have children ask a library media specialist to help them find current information about celestial bodies.

7. Stars do not live forever. Make a time line of the life cycle of a star. To do this, use the following information about the life of a star: As a star ages, its color shifts from yellowish to red, and the star expands to the red giant phase. It then contracts again. This is known as the white dwarf stage, which burns out slowly until the star dies.

8. Have children try these activities to increase their knowledge of space:

   a. A current theory about the universe that receives much attention is that the universe is expanding in size. That means that the distance between objects in the universe is increasing in all directions. To simulate an expanding universe, have children do the following: Randomly mark a plain, white balloon with about 20 dots using a marker (see fig. 15.2). Stand in front of a mirror and blow up the balloon, observing what happens to the dots. As the balloon swells, what happens to the distance between the spots? What can be concluded about how the universe changes as it expands?

Fig. 15.2. The Expanding Universe.

b. Because Earth is rotating, stars appear to rotate (as a group) when observed for several hours. To simulate the apparent rotation of the stars: Using a pin, poke about 10 small holes into a six-inch circle of black paper (see fig. 15.3). Stick the point of a pencil completely through the center of the circle and shine a flashlight on the circle while twirling the pencil between your hands. This will create an appearance of rings of light.

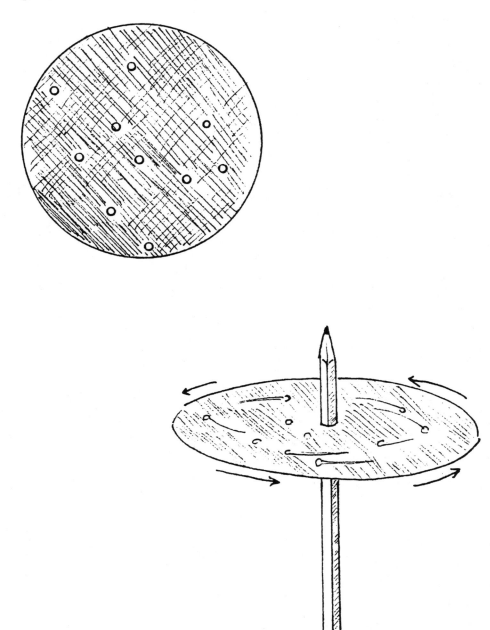

Fig. 15.3. Rotating Stars.

c. Make a shoe box planetarium: Cut off the end of a shoe box. At the opposite end of the box, cut a hole into which a flashlight will snugly fit. Using a pin, poke out the image of a constellation on a piece of black paper; tape the paper to the open end of the box. Darken the room, turn on the flashlight, and aim the box at a blank wall to see the constellation.

Make several constellations to share with classmates. Can they guess the constellations? NOTE: This activity should be done under supervision as sharp objects will be involved in the making of the planetarium. Flashlights should not be shown into children's eyes.

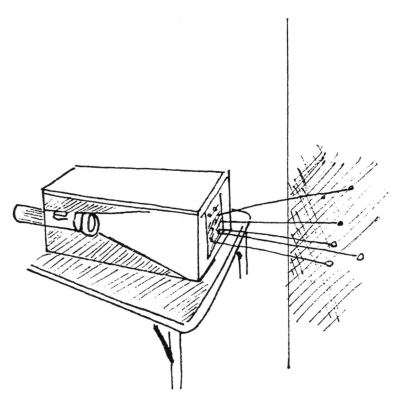

Fig. 15.4. Shoe Box Planetarium.

9. The invention of the telescope made possible a new age in space study. In the library media center, have children research the telescope, from the first telescopes through the Hubble space telescope. Can children explain how the lenses in the telescope magnify objects in space? NOTE: The invention of the telescope is attributed to Galileo in the early seventeenth century.

10. To discover things in space and then relay information about them to others takes great observational skills and the ability to communicate well with others. Have children practice these skills—observation and communication—by choosing particular spots in the classroom and describing them well enough for others to locate them.

11. In *My Place in Space*, Henry gave a very complete answer to the question, "Where do you live?" Besides having a list of places in space like Henry did, each of us also has many addresses on Earth. Some are formal addresses, such as "117 Concord Street, Indiana, PA

15701." Others are informal addresses, such as "in the Monticello development" or "near the mall." Ask children to think of various addresses that would help a newcomer to the school find their home.

12. Have children see how well they can guide someone to their house by writing out the directions. They should use landmarks, street names, and any shortcuts that might make it easier to find their house, and draw a map to accompany the directions.

13. Have children learn more about where they live on Earth by studying its landform divisions. Using a globe, have them find the equator, which divides Earth into the Northern and Southern Hemispheres. Which continents and oceans are in the Northern Hemisphere? Which continents and oceans are in the Southern Hemisphere? Have children find the prime meridian, which passes through Greenwich, England, and divides Earth into the Eastern and Western Hemispheres. Which continents and oceans are in the Eastern Hemisphere? Which continents and oceans are in the Western Hemisphere?

14. The United States is located in the Northern and the Western Hemispheres. Using a globe, have children locate the two hemispheres in which each of these cities is located: Buenos Aires, Argentina; Lima, Peru; Cairo, Egypt; Johannesburg, Union of South Africa; London, England; Moscow, Russia (the former U.S.S.R. is now called the Commonwealth of Independent States); and Sydney, Australia.

15. Have children show their mastery of hemispheres by selecting the name of two hemispheres and asking a partner to name any city that is located in these two hemispheres (e.g., the Northern and Eastern Hemispheres would include any cities in Europe, western Asia, and northern Africa). NOTE: Globes are easier to use for this activity, but flat desk maps may be much more accessible and convenient. However, avoid desk maps with the continents of North America and South America at the center of the map because this divides the Eastern Hemisphere into two sections and may confuse children.

16. Have children write their complete Earth address, including the following:

Street address

Neighborhood

School district

Township or city

County

Postal-code zone

Area code

State

Region

Country or nation

Continent

Hemisphere

Earth or Planet

17. Electronic addresses are commonly used today. Have children talk to a school secretary about how much electronic mail is received by and sent from the office. What persons in the office have e-mail accounts? What are the advantages of e-mail? What are the disadvantages?

18. Electronic addresses have a structure: the user name, the @ sign, and the service subscribed to. Have children analyze this e-mail address: jwbutzow@grove.iup.edu.

19. Have children learn to write proper addresses for physical addresses (i.e., home or business), as well as for electronic addresses. Discuss the reasons why people still write traditional letters instead of using e-mail.

20. Three Internet addresses can help children locate information for this unit of study:

    a. To access Earth and space science information, have children try this Internet address: http://www.windows.umich.edu.

    b. To access photos taken by the Hubble space telescope, have children try this Internet address: http://nssdc.gsfc.nasa.gov/photo gallery.

    c. To learn more about the U.S. space program, have children access Spacelink, an Internet information source about the U.S. space program, at http://spacelink.msfo.nasa.gov.

21. Crossword—Galaxies

CLUES

Across

5. Space beyond the limits of a celestial body (two words)
7. Object that orbits a planet
11. Galaxy containing our planet (two words)
12. All existing things
13. Instrument for studying celestial objects and bodies

Down

1. Diffused mass of interstellar dust and gas
2. Person who studies celestial objects and bodies
3. Celestial body with a tail and an elliptical orbit
4. Glowing ball of gas
6. Grouping of galaxies
8. Distance light travels in one year (two words)
9. Celestial body illuminated by the star around which it orbits
10. Celestial objects that orbit the Sun; they may be fragments of a planet

WORDS USED

asteroids
astronomer
comet
light year
Milky Way

moon
nebula
outer space
planet

star
supercluster
telescope
universe

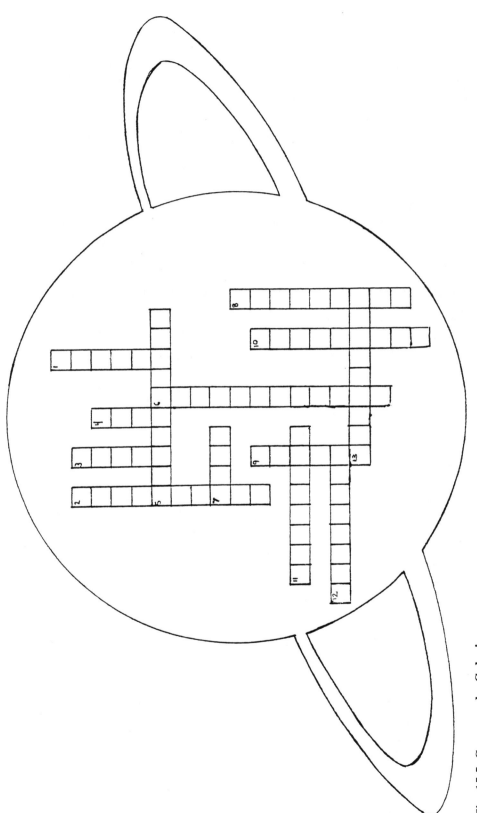

Fig. 15.5. Crossword—Galaxies.

Related Books and References

Banks, Dale A., and Harry D. Powell. "The Three Dimensional Universe." *The Science Teacher* 59, no. 7 (October 1992): 15–17.

Caduto, Michael J., and Joseph Bruchac. *Keepers of the Animals*. Golden, CO: Fulcrum Publishing, 1992.

Caduto, Michael J., and Joseph Bruchac. *Keepers of the Earth*. Golden, CO: Fulcrum Publishing, 1988.

Cole, Joanna. *The Magic School Bus Lost in the Solar System*. New York: Scholastic, 1990.

Holst, Gustav. *The Planets*. Boston Symphony Orchestra. Seiji Ozawa.

Hunn, Diana. "Constellations, Slide by Slide." *Science and Children* 29, no. 7 (April 1992): 15.

Kepler, Lynne. "Finding North." *Science and Children* 31, no. 4 (January 1994): 46.

Livingston, Myra Cohn. *Space Songs*. New York: Holiday House, 1988.

Reston, James, Jr. "Orion: Where Stars Are Born." *National Geographic* 188, no. 6 (December 1995): 90–101.

Small, Larry. "The Earth Is a Peppercorn." *Science and Children* 29, no. 7 (April 1992): 51.

Uslabar, Kenneth M. "A Stroll Through the Solar System." *Science Scope* 17, no. 2 (October 1993): 41–43.

Van Cleave, Janice. *Astronomy for Every Kid: 101 Easy Experiments That Really Work*. New York: John Wiley, 1991.

Whitney, David. "The Case of the Misplaced Planets." *Science and Children* 32, no. 5 (February 1995): 12–14+.

Part III
Physical Science and Technology

Chapter 16

Force, Motion, and Music

Berlioz the Bear

by Jan Brett
New York: G. P. Putnam's Sons, 1991

Summary

On their way to a concert in the village, the musicians are suddenly struck by disaster as the wagon hits a pothole in the road. Fortunately, the giant sting of a randomly passing bee convinces the mule to accelerate the wagon out of its trap, and the musicians arrive at the concert on time.

Science and Content Related Concepts

Acceleration, force, sound

Content Related Words

Motion, effort, push/pull, vibration, inertia, acceleration, momentum, mass, rest

Activities

1. *Berlioz the Bear* takes place in the mountains of an unnamed European country. Using an atlas, have children investigate which countries in Europe have tall mountains. In the library media center, have children research these countries, locating pictures of native folk costumes, too, if possible. What countries could possibly be the setting of the story? What is the geography of the country? How would life be different if the children lived there?

2. Berlioz the Bear was named after a famous French composer. Have children research this man using an encyclopedia or music dictionary. What can they learn about him? Why do they think Berlioz the Bear was named after this famous composer? Have children listen to *Symphonie Fantastique*, one of Hector Berlioz's more famous works.

3. Instruments of the orchestra belong to four categories—strings, brasses, woodwinds, and percussion (see fig. 16.1). Ask the music teacher to visit the classroom and play an instrument from each category (e.g., a violin, a French horn, a clarinet, and a drum). Ask the music teacher to explain and demonstrate how sound is produced by vibration. What is the relationship of vibration to producing higher and lower notes? What distinctive sound quality marks instruments of each category?

Fig. 16.1. Musical Instruments.

4. To learn more about the instruments of the orchestra, have children listen to *Peter and the Wolf* by the Russian composer Sergey Prokofiev. Can children identify the characters in the piece by the instruments that represent them?

5. The words *largo* and *encore* (from French) are music terms. In *Berlioz the Bear*, the mule's name is Largo, and the audience shouts "Encore!" after Berlioz plays his string bass. Using a dictionary, have children find the meanings of these words, which have become part of the English language. Or, have children ask the music teacher to help them learn a variety of music terms (e.g., *piano* for "soft"; *forte* for "loud"; *subito* for "suddenly").

6. Rhythm is an essential quality that musicians should possess. Guide children in clapping various rhythms that are fast, slow, and syncopated (e.g., slow, fast, fast, slow, fast, fast, rest).

7. If the class members can read music, have them clap the rhythms of songs in the text book that they use in music class. Have children pay attention to the time values of whole notes, half notes, quarter notes, eighth notes, and sixteenth notes. Try singing songs accompanied by a drum-type rhythm different than the rhythm of the melody of the song. As children learn to do this, add more rhythms.

8. Have children look at the picture on the last page of *Berlioz the Bear*, in which Berlioz is playing the string bass. The music is called "The Flight of the Bumblebee" by Nikolay Rimsky-Korsakov. Ask children to name the kinds of notes they see. How fast do they think this piece is being played? What would the piece sound like? Have children listen to a recording of "The Flight of the Bumblebee" to see if they have guessed correctly.

9. Have children use a ramp (a guttered ruler works well) and a large marble to move a small box containing varying amounts of weight (see fig. 16.2). Rest one end of the ramp on a book to maintain a uniform slope. After each trial, increase the amount of weight in the box. Does the box eventually become too heavy for the marble to move it? Why does this happen?

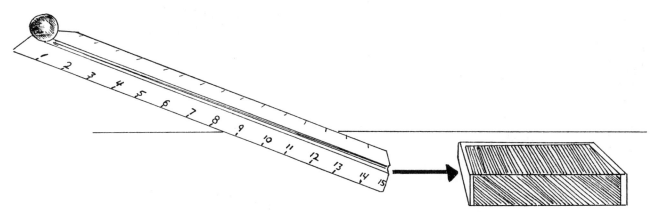

Fig. 16.2. Ramp and Marble.

Have children increase the slope of the ramp. What effect does this have on the marble's capacity to move the box? Have children compare this experiment to *Berlioz the Bear*, when the mule was stung by the bee and lurched forward. Why was the mule able to pull the wagon out of the mud after it was stung by a bee? NOTE: Force depends upon both weight (mass) and acceleration. The wagon moved because the mule suddenly moved (accelerated) after it was stung, thereby pulling on the wagon with greater force.

10. Have children repeat activity 9 using a small wind-up truck with a spring that can be wound to variable degrees of tightness. Begin with a small amount of sand in the truck, increasing the amount of sand with each attempt, but without varying the tightness to which the spring is wound. Does the sand eventually become too heavy for the truck to move? Next, maintain the same amount of sand, but increase the tightness of the spring with each attempt. How does the tightness of the spring affect the movement of the truck? Which makes more of a difference—varying the tightness of the spring, or varying the amount of sand in the truck?

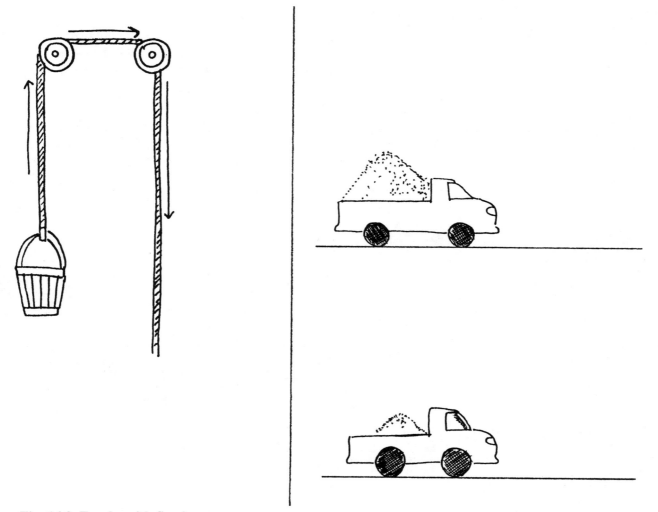

Fig. 16.3. Trucks with Sand.

11. In the story, when the wagon stops, the animals in the wagon continue to move forward a bit. Ask children why they think this is so. On the school playground, have children investigate this phenomenon: Fill a toy wheelbarrow or wagon with water. Push the wheelbarrow or wagon along swiftly, then stop it suddenly. What happens to the water? NOTE: This tendency for objects in motion to remain in motion is known as the law of inertia (one of Isaac Newton's three laws of motion). This law also specifies that an object at rest tends to remain at rest. Have children demonstrate this by placing an object on a sheet of paper and quickly pulling the paper from beneath the object. The object will remain in place. Magicians and comedians often do this with a tablecloth and a set of dishes, which remain in place when the tablecloth is pulled from beneath the dishes.

12. In the story, larger and larger animals failed to move the wagon. Ask children why the animals failed. What would children do to move an object that is stuck?

13. Seat belts are a means of explaining how the law of inertia works. When the car stops, the person is thrown forward but is held in place by the seat belt. Why should persons in a car wear seat belts? What keeps the passenger from moving forward when the car stops? In the story, what happened to the animals in the wagon when the wagon stopped? If children were to design a wagon that would not lurch forward when stopping, would it be better to have the seats facing forwards, backwards, or sideways? Have children apply this knowledge to the design of infant and toddler car seats.

14. In the story, there is at least one other way that the wagon could have been freed. Have children brainstorm possibilities that might have worked for the musicians, and then rewrite the ending of the story.

15. Have children write an alternate ending for the story in which the wagon is not freed from the pothole. What would have happened to the musicians in this scenario?

16. Have children pretend that they are wagon makers living in the village with Berlioz and the musicians. By using drawings, have them show how they would make the "special-order" wagons listed below. Variables might include number of axles, number of wheels, position of the load, and so on. Ask a library media specialist to help children find pictures of antique wagons (see fig. 16.4) to help them invent the following wagons:

    For the king and queen to use in elegant parades

    For the miners to haul coal

    For the farmers to haul hay to the barn

    For a family of four to go visiting on Sunday

    For the father to haul firewood

    For the dairyman to deliver milk

    For the mother to bring goods home from the market

    For a horse to pull satchels and backpacks for one traveler

    For the fireman to bring water to a flame

    For the cobbler to visit his customers

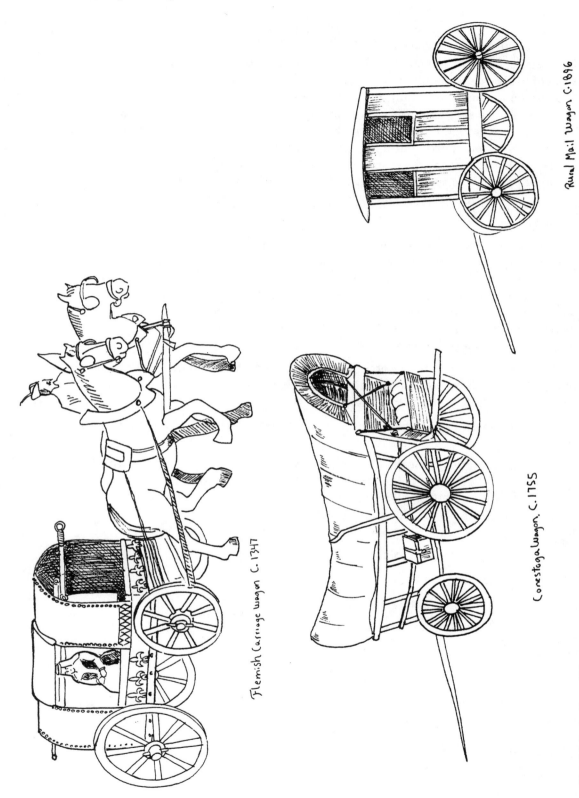

Flemish Carriage Wagon c. 1347

Rural Mail Wagon c. 1896

Conestoga Wagon c. 1755

Fig. 16.4. Antique Wagons.

From *More Science Through Children's Literature.* © 1998 Butzow and Butzow. Teacher Ideas Press. (800) 237-6124.

17. Have children pretend that they are the mayor of the village where Berlioz and the musicians played their concert. Have children write a letter to Berlioz telling him what a wonderful job the musicians did, and perhaps commenting on their misfortune during their journey to the village.

18. For additional activities about music, see Chapter 18, "Sound and Music."

19. Word Scramble—Orchestra Instruments
    Names of orchestra instruments are given below in scrambled form. To help you, the instruments are listed by the category to which they belong.

CLUES

Strings

a. lionvi

b. sabs

c. aliov

d. leclo

Woodwinds

i. ooeb

j. tinclare

k. sligneh rohn

l. xaoshopne

Brass

e. prettum

f. toneborm

g. chefrn rohn

h. buta

Percussion

m. smrud

n. oanip

o. slebl

WORDS USED

bass	English horn	trombone
bells	French horn	trumpet
cello	oboe	tuba
clarinet	piano	viola
drums	saxophone	violin

Related Books and References

Anthony, Joan L. "Race Car Rally." *Science and Children* 31, no. 5 (February 1994): 26–29.

Berlioz, Hector. *Symphonie Fantastique.* Boston Symphony Orchestra. Charles Munch.

Prokofiev, Sergey. *Peter and the Wolf.* New York: Viking, 1982.

Prokofiev, Sergey. *Peter and the Wolf.* Royal Philharmonic Orchestra. Andre Previn.

Rimsky-Korsakov, Nikolay. "The Flight of the Bumblebee." From *Tale of Tsar Saltana Suite.* Philadelphia Orchestra. Joseph Ormandy.

Chapter 17

The Ice Industry

The Ice Horse

by Candace Christiansen
New York: Dial Books for Young Readers, 1993

Summary

There was a time when men and horses worked together as a team to complete the ice harvest. They would wait until the ice was two feet thick, then saw out huge blocks of ice, which was stored beneath layers of sawdust. This ice was sold in the city during the hot days of summer.

Science and Content Related Concepts

Ice harvest, physical change, seasons, ice as a coolant

Content Related Words

Freezing, ice house, ice saw, horse shoes, friction, channel, conveyor belt, sawdust

Activities

1. Have children orient themselves to the setting of this story by locating the Hudson River, in eastern New York state, on a map (see fig. 17.1). Which mountains lie to the west of this river? Which mountains lie to the north? Name another large New York river that was the site of the ice harvesting industry. What city at the mouth of the Hudson River was a market for the ice blocks that Jack in *The Ice Horse* helped harvest?

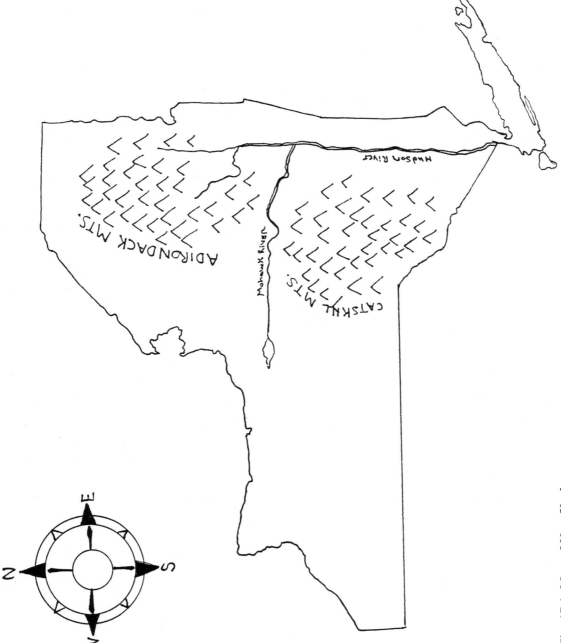

Fig. 17.1. Map of New York.

From *More Science Through Children's Literature.* © 1998 Butzow and Butzow. Teacher Ideas Press. (800) 237-6124.

2. *The Ice Horse* was illustrated by Thomas Locker. So that children might appreciate the landscape and scenery of the Hudson River Valley and other nearby locations, have a library media specialist help them locate additional books illustrated by Thomas Locker, such as *Where the River Begins.*

3. Water is one of the few compounds that humans can comfortably observe in its solid, liquid, and gaseous states (see fig. 17.2). Have children list the properties or characteristics that describe water in each of these three states.

4. Have children try this experiment: Fill two identical, plastic drinking glasses approximately two-thirds full with warm water (about 100 degrees Fahrenheit). Using a thermometer, have children verify that the temperatures of the water samples are equal. Pour one-quarter cup of cold water into one glass; put two or three ice cubes into the other glass. Let the ice cubes melt, then have children measure again the temperatures of the water samples. Which is colder? Why? NOTE: The glass to which the ice was added is colder because the ice, requiring heat to melt, drew heat from the water. Ice cools water more than an equivalent amount of cold water.

5. To understand the purpose of using sawdust in the ice harvesting industry, have children try this experiment: Put two or three ice cubes into each of two plastic containers (e.g., butter tubs or whipped topping containers) (see fig. 17.3). In one container, completely cover the ice cubes with sawdust, to the top of the container. Have children record the time for the ice cubes to melt in each container. What can they conclude about the insulating qualities of sawdust?

6. Have children try the experiment in activity 5 again, using various other materials to cover or wrap the ice cubes in one of the containers (e.g., sand, soil, Styrofoam pellets, fabric, aluminum foil, plastic wrap). What can they conclude? Which material would be of most use in manufacturing winter clothing? How could a home be best insulated? Which material could be used to keep food cool at the beach? NOTE: Always use a second container of uncovered or unwrapped ice cubes as a "control" against which to compare the experiment.

7. Have children try this experiment: Place an ice cube into a glass of cool water. Notice that it floats. Place several coins onto the ice cube until it begins to sink. Why does this happen? Remove the coins and note the result. What can children conclude about the relative weight of an amount of ice and the same amount of water? What happens if warm water or salt water is used?

8. An ice saw was used to cut the blocks of ice from the river. Have children make a saw from a wire hanger and string or dental floss (see fig. 17.4) to cut ice cubes. Have children hold an ice cube in a towel so that the top of it is exposed. Set the string (or dental floss) on the ice cube and begin to saw, slowly. What happens to the ice? Saw quickly. What happens now? What force is really "sawing" the ice cube? Why is a metal ice saw more practical for cutting ice than a string ice saw? NOTE: It is important to consider the relationship between friction and heat in sawing the ice.

Fig. 17.2. Water as Solid, Liquid, and Gas.

Fig. 17.3. Sawdust as Insulation.

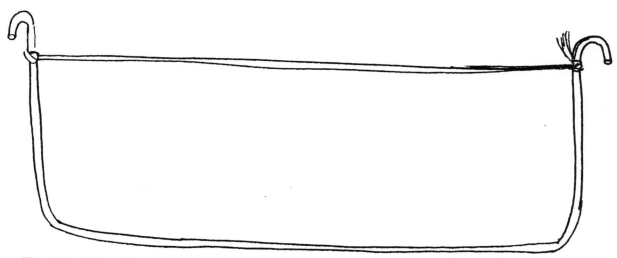

Fig. 17.4. String Saw.

9. Have children design and make an icebox from cardboard boxes or shoe boxes that will effectively hold enough ice to refrigerate food without the use of electricity. Where should the food be placed to effectively keep it cold—above or below the ice? What happens as the ice melts, and what should the children do to collect the water that develops? How is an icebox different from a refrigerator-freezer combination appliance? Is there a museum or another place where one might see an old-fashioned icebox? Have children test the icebox using a dish of ice cubes or a small block of ice.

10. Using the pictures in *The Ice Horse* as a guide, have children indicate which stages of the ice harvest were made easier by the use of simple machines. NOTE: The simple machines may be combined to make a new implement or they can be used separately.

11. To remember the names of the six simple machines shown in *The Ice Horse* (see fig. 17.5), have children devise a mnemonic device in which the first letters of the words in a phrase represent the first letters of the words to be remembered (e.g., "Willie Anderson was probably lost somewhere in Pittsburgh" stands for the six simple machines **w**heel and **a**xle, **w**edge, **p**ulley, **l**ever, **s**crew, and **i**nclined **p**lane).

12. Have children compare ice harvesting to the logging, farming, and mining industries to determine which industries do not harm the environment. Ask these questions:

    Is the product renewable?

    What resources must be used to obtain the product?

    What is the cost of production?

    What is the effect on the environment of obtaining the product?

    Have children rank these four industries from least harmful to most harmful. Ask children to think of and evaluate other industries. How do these industries rank with the original four?

13. Have children talk to older people in the community about ice harvesting and keeping perishable foods cold before the advent of refrigeration. From where was ice obtained? Was it possible to get ice in southern states, where it is relatively warm all year? Were there other "old-fashioned" industries from the same time period that flourished in your community but have since disappeared (e.g., blacksmithing, barrel making)? If possible, invite people who knew these industries to visit the class and speak about them.

14. The icebox was used to keep perishable foods fresh for several days. Ask children if they know of other methods of food preservation that were used during the time period of *The Ice Horse*? Compare these methods to the methods used today. Have children list the ways in which their life and their diet would be different if they were living during the time period of the story.

15. Jack and Max were a part of the ice harvesting team. Ask children who or what comprised the rest of the team? What were the steps of the ice harvest as performed by this team? How did teamwork make the ice harvesting process more efficient and faster? When are teams especially useful in the classroom? What jobs are better done by teams rather than individual children?

16. In 1891, the cost of ice (including delivery) was $.50 a week for an average family. The average wage of ice workers was $1.50 per week. Have children calculate how much of this weekly wage was needed to provide refrigeration for an average family? How does this compare to today's cost of running an electric refrigerator for one week? NOTE: These figures are from Jeffrey J. Miller's book *The Iceman Cameth*, as quoted in the *Olean Times Herald*, Olean, NY, on June 18, 1996. Sears appliance center states that the current cost of running a refrigerator-freezer for one year averages $60 per year or about $1 per week.

17. The men in the story were farmers who cut ice during the "off season." Have children identify professions that today are seasonal in nature (e.g., hockey player, roofing contractor).

18. Ice and snow are positive occurrences in *The Ice Horse*. Have children write about a time in their life when ice or snow was a benefit to them or when it was a problem (e.g., slipping on the ice and breaking an arm).

19. Have the children look up additional information on the Internet using keywords "ice harvesting."

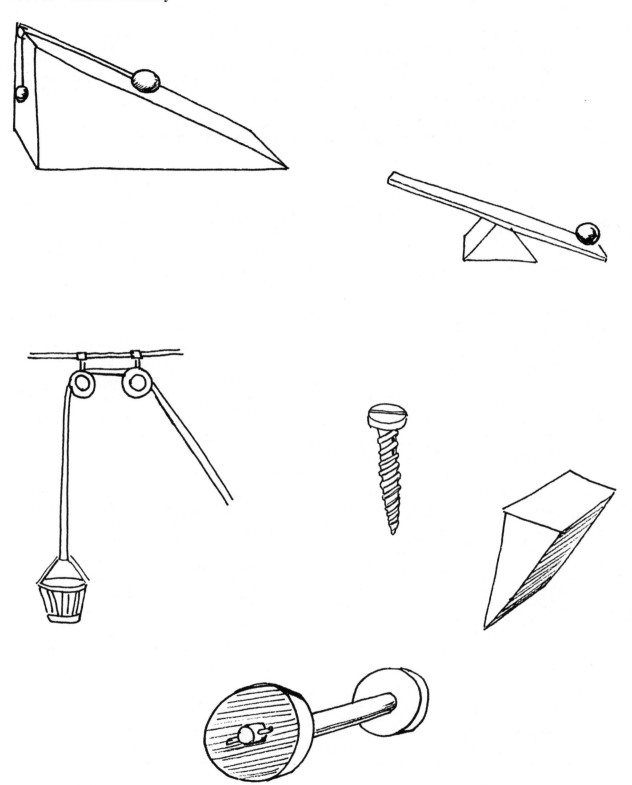

Fig. 17.5. Simple Machines.

From *More Science Through Children's Literature*. © 1998 Butzow and Butzow. Teacher Ideas Press. (800) 237-6124.

20. Following are 12 steps in the ice harvesting process. Have children work in groups to arrange the steps into a workable order (from 1 to 12). Have groups compare answers. Are the lists identical? Is there only one correct answer? Are there any incorrect answers? Why might there be variations in the answers? NOTE: Many steps were done repeatedly, such as "Row boats in the channels to keep them open." So a step's position in the order can vary.

_____ .   Take sawdust to the ice house.

_____ .   Cut channels in the ice.

_____ .   Load the ice onto conveyor belts.

_____ .   Sell the ice to customers.

_____ .   Wait for the river to freeze to a depth of about two feet.

_____ .   Row boats in the channels to keep them open.

_____ .   Stack the ice in the ice house.

_____ .   Take the ice by wagon to the railroad.

_____ .   Bring in farmers to help with the harvest.

_____ .   Pole the ice through the open channels.

_____ .   Cut the ice into large blocks.

_____ .   Cover the ice with sawdust for storage.

21. Word Matching—Simple Machines

People use simple machines of many forms. Listed below are examples of six simple machines. (Each example may be a combination of more than one simple machine.) Select two examples to represent each type of simple machine. Each example may be used only once.

EXAMPLES

auto jack	corkscrew	ramp
ax	crowbar	shovel
baseball bat	flagpole	wagon
bicycle	playground slide	drapery pull

SIMPLE MACHINES

Wheel and Axle

a. _____

b. _____

Lever

c. _____

d. _____

Wedge

e. _____

f. _____

Inclined Plane

g. _____

h. _____

Pulley

i. _____

j. _____

Screw

k. _____

l. _____

Related Books and References

Locker, Thomas. *Where the River Begins*. New York: Dial Books for Young Readers, 1984.

Melville, Herman. *Catskill Eagle*. Illus. by Thomas Locker. New York: Philomel, 1991.

Young, Janet. "Complex Creations from Simple Machines." *The Science Teacher* 61, no. 1 (January 1994): 16–19.

Chapter 18

Sound and Music

Ty's One Man Band

by Mildred Pitts Walter
New York: Four Winds Press, 1980

Summary

It was a hot, sultry day and Ty had nothing to do except lie in the tall grass by the pond. There he met a man who had a peg leg. The man introduced himself as Andro, the one man band. No one believed Ty when he told them that Andro would come that evening to entertain them. True to his word, Andro played for the townsfolk, and everyone danced in the streets before Andro quietly slipped away into the night.

Science and Content Related Concepts

Sound, vibration, rhythm, musical instrument, Railroad Age, Orff instruments

Content Related Words

Hobo (tramp), peg leg, juggle, one man band, vibration, pitch

Activities

1. Sound is produced when air is made to vibrate against an object. Have children determine the various ways that sound can be produced. Have a box of potential sound-makers ready for the children, such as plastic jars, bottles and lids, boxes, pencils, rubber bands, rulers, wooden spoons, and other kitchen utensils (see fig. 18.1). Include various sizes of each object (different sizes produce different sounds). Have children describe the sounds produced. Can different sounds be produced using the same sound-maker?

2. Have children classify the sound-makers in the box according to how the sound is produced—blown, plucked, strummed, or struck. What musical instruments do the sound-makers resemble? Have children compare the characteristics of the various sounds produced.

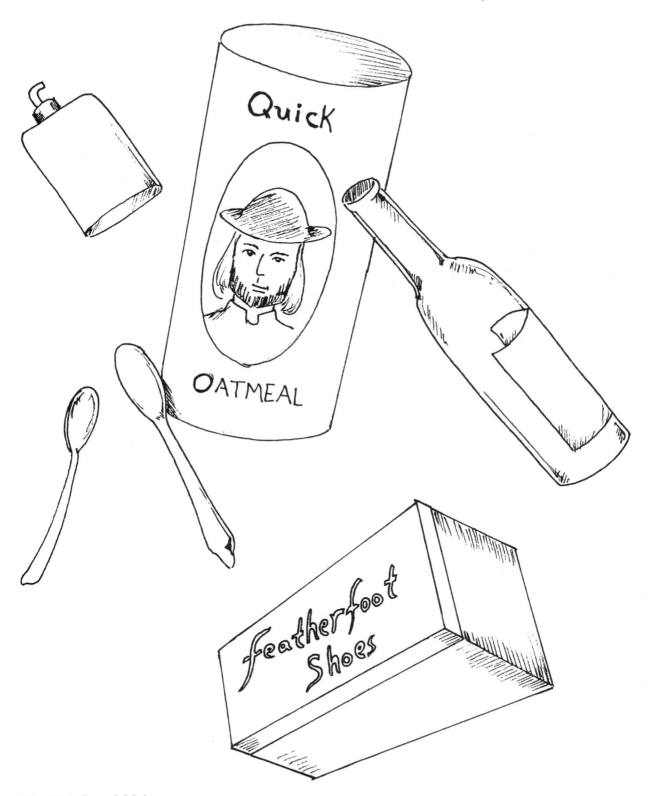

Fig. 18.1. Sound-Makers.

From *More Science Through Children's Literature.* © 1998 Butzow and Butzow. Teacher Ideas Press. (800) 237-6124.

3. Using the sound-makers, have children experiment and determine how to make a sound deeper or higher. NOTE: Generally, the bigger the object, the deeper the sound.

4. Have children stretch a rubber band across a hole cut in a container (e.g., in the lid of a shoe box or in the side of a dish soap container). Pluck the rubber band with one finger while sliding the other finger in each direction along the rubber band. When is the note highest? When is it lowest? What can children conclude from this experiment about producing sounds using an instrument?

5. Have children make a set of instruments following the directions below. With these instruments, is it possible to become a one man band? Ask children to suggest other everyday items that can serve as musical instruments, such as plastic pipes (flutes), sticks (maracas), pizza pans (cymbals), and toy wooden blocks (percussion).

Sand Blocks

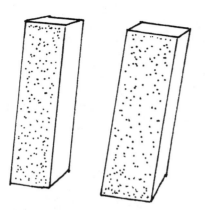

a. Cover one side of each of two small wooden blocks with sandpaper (see fig. 18.2).

b. Rub the sandpapered sides together in a circular motion to produce a "sandy" percussive effect.

Ask children how the sound is produced. What happens when the sandpapered sides are rubbed together in a different manner? Is there any other way to produce sounds with wooden blocks? Does the amount of pressure exerted make a difference?

Fig. 18.2. Sand Blocks.

Water Scale

a. Line up eight identical glasses or bottles.

b. Fill each glass or bottle to a different level, beginning with a nearly full glass and decreasing the level of water level until the last glass is nearly empty (see fig. 18.3).

c. Lightly tap the tops of the glasses or bottles, or blow across the openings.

d. Adjust water levels to produce an eight-tone scale.

Ask children how they adjusted the water levels to change the tones of the scale. What happened to the pitch of the note when water was added? How was the pitch affected when water was removed?

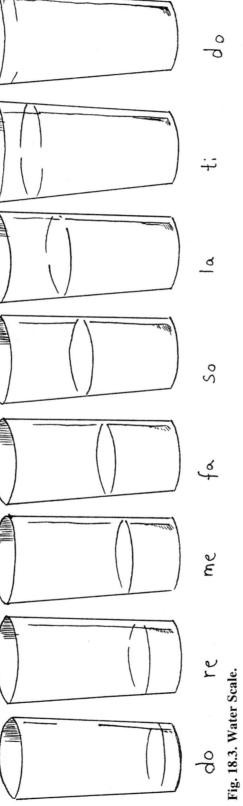

Fig. 18.3. Water Scale.

Rubber Band Guitar

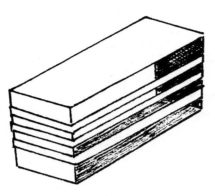

a. Place three different-sized rubber bands lengthwise around the box, so that they do not touch one another (see fig. 18.4).

b. Pluck the rubber bands gently, one at a time, then two at a time, then all three together.

Ask children why the sound created by each rubber band is different. What happens when plucking more than one of the rubber bands together? What happens when plucking a rubber band while pressing it with your finger against the box? What causes the difference in sound? How else might sounds be produced?

Fig. 18.4. Rubber Band Guitar.

Comb/Paper Kazoo

a. Cover a small pocket comb with waxed paper (see fig. 18.5).

b. Have children hum onto the paper to produce music.

Ask children how this instrument produces sound. What is the source of the vibration? Is there any way to make the sounds higher or lower?

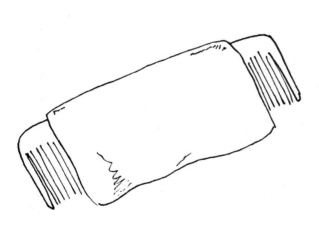

Fig. 18.5. Comb/Paper Kazoo.

Coffee Can Drum/Shaker

a. Put dried beans or peas, macaroni, unpopped popcorn, or sand into an empty coffee can (see fig. 18.6).

b. Place the plastic lid on the can or cover it with paper or cloth that is held in place by a rubber band.

c. Tap the top of the can or shake the can to produce music.

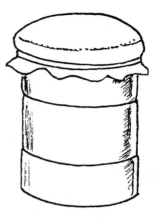

Ask children which part of this instrument vibrates. What is the difference between sound produced by tapping the can and sound produced by shaking it? Place the same amount of material (beans, etc.) into a different-sized coffee can. Is there a difference between the sounds produced by the cans when they are tapped? When they are shaken? Is a different sound produced if different materials are put into the can? How do the sounds produced by larger or smaller drums compare to the sounds produced by the original coffee can? NOTE: To make

Fig. 18.6. Coffee Can Drum/Shaker.

a smaller drum/shaker, use a potato-chip canister; secure the top to the can with masking tape. To make a larger drum/shaker, use an oatmeal box or a large potato-chip or coffee can.

6. To better feel vibrations produced by sound, have children put their ears against a desk while lightly tapping their fingers on the desk. Compare the sound produced when listening with the ear against the desk to the sound produced when listening without touching the ear to the desk. How does this relate to old cowboy movies in which people put their ears against the ground to hear movement of animals or people or other loud noises?

7. To "see" vibration produced by sound, have children put unpopped popcorn or rice on top of a drum or an oatmeal box and lightly tap the top of the drum or box. The popcorn will bounce. Another way to see the effects of vibration is to strike a tuning fork and plunge it into water. What can children conclude about the nature of vibration? How else might vibration be seen? Another way to "see" vibration is to put a small amount of dry rice on a paper plate, then place the plate on a loudly playing radio.

8. Have children make a string telephone, which works by transforming sound into vibration, then back into sound. To make a string telephone:

a. Using a pencil, poke a hole in the bottom of two Styrofoam cups.

b. Cut a four-yard length of string; push the ends of the string into the bottom of each cup (see fig. 18.7).

c. Secure the string to the insides of the cups with tape.

d. Talk into a cup while a partner holds the other cup to their ear.

e. Reverse roles.

Ask children how the sound moved from one cup to the other. What happens if the string is touched while talking on the string telephone? Can the "volume" be adjusted? How long can the string be before the voice cannot be received on the other end?

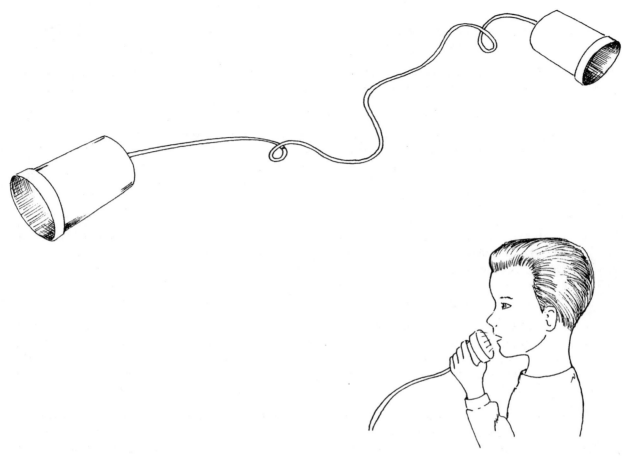

Fig. 18.7. String Telephone.

9. Ask children to name everyday sounds. Divide the class into groups; give each a portable cassette recorder. Have children record sounds heard in and outside the classroom. Have groups exchange cassettes and try to identify the sounds. Have interested children record sounds heard outside the classroom (e.g., at a soccer match after school, in the kitchen at home while everyone is getting ready to go to work and school).

10. Have children listen to a cassette of sound effects (available at record stores). Sounds might include common noises, such as a door closing or a car horn honking. After children can quickly identify these sounds, have each child record himself or herself telling a story. Children should include self-made sound effects as an accompaniment to their story.

11. A study unit on sound provides a good opportunity to work with the music teacher. Arrange for the demonstration and use of various Orff instruments, band instruments, piano, and guitar. Have children determine how each sound is produced—blown, plucked, strummed, or struck. Is a combination of actions necessary to produce different notes? NOTE: This demonstration might be done by upper-grade children for those in the lower grades as an introduction to the band and orchestra programs.

12. Have children play a piano with the top or front of the piano open so the action of the keys and strings can be observed. What causes the strings to vibrate? What dampens their vibrations? What is the relationship between string length and pitch? What causes the volume to change?

13. To learn more about the instruments of the orchestra, have children listen to the orchestral piece *Peter and the Wolf* by Sergey Prokofiev. Can children identify the characters in the piece by the instruments that represent them?

14. Not only does music consist of notes, it includes the use of rhythms—the time sequences of the notes. Guide children in clapping rhythms that are fast, slow, and syncopated (e.g., slow, fast, fast, slow, fast, fast, rest). Clap rhythms that have a different number of beats to each interval or measure (e.g., clap, rest, clap, clap, rest, clap, clap). Have children compose and demonstrate rhythms.

15. Movement can be rhythmic in nature. Ask children if they can identify specific classmates by their footsteps. Have everyone close their eyes. Select one child (touch them on the shoulder) to walk around the room. Can the class identify the child? Can the class learn to identify all class members by their footsteps? Can children identify what people are doing by the rhythm of their movement and their sound effects?

16. Sound is important to animals because it helps them to find food. For this simulation, take the class to a grassy location free of trees and obstacles. Before beginning the activity, have the children set up some ground rules—no running, no pushing, etc. There should be one adult for every 8 to 10 students. Blindfold children and designate each as either predator (a bird) or prey (an insect). To play the game, birds say "cheep cheep;" insects say "click click." Children move around slowly, either hunting for prey or trying to avoid being caught. If a predator captures a prey, the prey is considered eaten and is out of the game. If two predators or two of the prey meet, they are considered safe and continue playing. It is not permissible for prey to attack each other, nor can prey "eat" a predator. For predators, the object of the game is to successfully capture prey; for prey, to avoid being caught until the end of the game. The time allotted for one round of the game should be about one to two minutes. Play several rounds of the game to give each child a chance to be both predator and prey.

17. In the story, Ty's sister made cornbread. Have children try this recipe for cornbread or cornmeal muffins:

> ¼ cup softened margarine
> ½ cup sugar
> 2 eggs
> 1 cup milk
> 2 cups flour
> 1 cup cornmeal
> 1 tablespoon plus 1 teaspoon baking powder
> ½ teaspoon salt

Cream margarine and sugar in a large bowl. Add eggs and milk; mix. Add the remaining ingredients; mix. Pour into a greased 8"x8" or 6"x9" baking pan or a 12-count muffin tin. Bake at 400 degrees Fahrenheit for 20 minutes.

18. The 1920s and 1930s produced a multitude of African American musicians whose music was influenced by the places they lived and the everyday events of their day. Ask the music teacher or someone from a local music shop to give a brief overview of the era and to play music of that time. Listen carefully to some of this music. What were some of the topics in this music?

19. In the story, Ty was influenced by Andro's music. Have children write a story about how Ty continues his interest in music as he grows older.

20. *Ty's One Man Band* is illustrated with silhouettes. Have children stand in front of a light to cast a profile shadow of their heads. On white paper, outline the shadows. Transfer the outlines to black paper and cut out the silhouettes. Have children identify their classmates by silhouette. Label the silhouettes and display them in the classroom or in a hallway.

Fig. 18.8. Silhouettes.

21. Math Puzzle

    Solve the arithmetic problems, then match the answers to the letter to decode the words. Correct answers will spell Andro's greeting to Ty.

A	B	C	D	E	F	G	H	I	J	K	L	M
1	2	3	4	5	6	7	8	9	10	11	12	13

N	O	P	Q	R	S	T	U	V	W	X	Y	Z
14	15	16	17	18	19	20	21	22	23	24	25	26

___ ___   ___ ___ ___ ___
10+3 5x5   7+7 0+1 7+6 2+3

___ ___   ___ ___ ___ ___ ___
4+5 7+12   3-2 9+5 2+2 9+9 7+8

___ ___   ___   ___ ___ ___
11-2 9+4   5-4   20-5 7x2 4+1

___ ___ ___   ___ ___ ___ ___
20-7 7-6 7x2   1+1 8-7 11+3 2x2

Related Books and References

Huetinck, Linda. "Physics to Beat the Band." *Science and Children* 32, no. 3 (November/December 1994): 27–30.

Prokofiev, Sergey. *Peter and the Wolf.* Royal Philharmonic Orchestra. Andre Previn.

Chapter 19

Machines and Power

Katy and the Big Snow

by Virginia Lee Burton
Boston: Houghton Mifflin, 1943

Summary

Katy, the snowplow, was so big and so strong that there was not enough snow for her to plow. Instead, she stayed in her garage—until the big snowstorm came. Only Katy was able to plow all that snow. After the streets of Geoppolis were clear, Katy went back to her garage for a well-deserved rest.

Science and Content Related Concepts

Machines, work power, horsepower, snow disaster, effects of snow, prioritization of decisions, geography of Geoppolis

Content Related Words

Superintendent, emergency, three-alarm fire, road maintenance, work, horsepower, snow removal, snow plow, bulldozer, crawler, tractor

Activities

1. Read aloud related books by Virginia Lee Burton, including *Mike Mulligan and His Steam Shovel*, *The Little House*, and *Choo Choo*. Have children discuss the role of machines in each story. Are machines shown in a positive or negative way? How do the machines contribute to the end of the story?

2. Katy does not plow the snow in a random fashion. She has specific priorities. Have children list, in order, the places or services that Katy plows. Which are plowed first? Which are left until the end? Are there other places or services that children would include? What would be on their list of priorities?

3. Katy was so strong because her engine had much horsepower, or the power of many horses. Figure 19.1 shows the horsepower of various machines, including a snowblower, chain saw, regular lawnmower, riding lawnmower, Rototiller, scroll saw, grinder, drill, garage door opener, router, circular saw, and table saw. Have children research the horsepower

of other machines, including a snow plow (if possible), using magazines and newspapers, car-dealer pamphlets, brochures about motorcycles, advertisements from farming supplies stores and tractor stores, and information from the Internet. Also, children may ask people involved in selling these machines, or people who have purchased these machines for themselves.

Have children ask their parents or others to help them research the horsepower for a compact car, a six-passenger car, an outboard motorboat, an inboard motorboat, a motorcycle, and a school bus. Have children make a horsepower chart for these machines.

4. Katy had two blades—one for bulldozing and one for plowing. Ask children to explain the differences between the blades. Using cardboard plows and a sand table, have children try to replicate Katy's two blades. Use the drawings of the snowplow to show a flat blade and a pointed blade.

5. A map of Geoppolis in the middle of *Katie and the Big Snow* is surrounded by pictures of businesses and services, some of which no longer exist (e.g., the piggery). Also, businesses and services that are common today did not exist at the time this story was written (e.g., television stations and computer repair services). Have children make a list of businesses and services under the headings "Then" and "Now." Have children ask their parents and grandparents to help them with the "Then" column—businesses and services that have become obsolete.

6. A service that has become obsolete is ice harvesting and delivery. For activities related to this enterprise, see Chapter 17, "The Ice Industry."

7. To understand how *work* is defined in physics, have children use a small pulley to lift objects of various weight (or weights of known mass). What can children conclude about how much work is being done by how difficult it is to move the various objects or weights. NOTE: Various sizes of pulleys can be purchased at hardware stores.

8. Children can experience the concept of work by pulling a sturdy wagon that contains increasingly heavy or light objects. Ask children what happens as weight is added to or removed from the wagon. How can children show that they are doing more work? Less work?

9. To express the work done using numbers, have the class repeat activity 8, but with children sitting in the wagon. The child who will be pulling the wagon should not look to see how many children are in the wagon. Have the child pull the wagon and estimate the number of children in the wagon. Repeat the experiment several times, changing the number of children in the wagon. Allow every child a chance to pull the wagon and estimate the load. If possible, do this activity in groups.

10. Power is the amount of work done per unit of time. In other words, more power is required to do the same amount of work in less time. Using two identical wind-up trucks, have children gradually increase the weight carried by one truck. What are the results? How can children explain the results? To vary this activity, have children use the trucks to push objects, carry objects, or pull objects. NOTE: Small boxes filled with sand work well for the cargo or load. NOTE: The second truck is used as a comparison or control in this experiment.

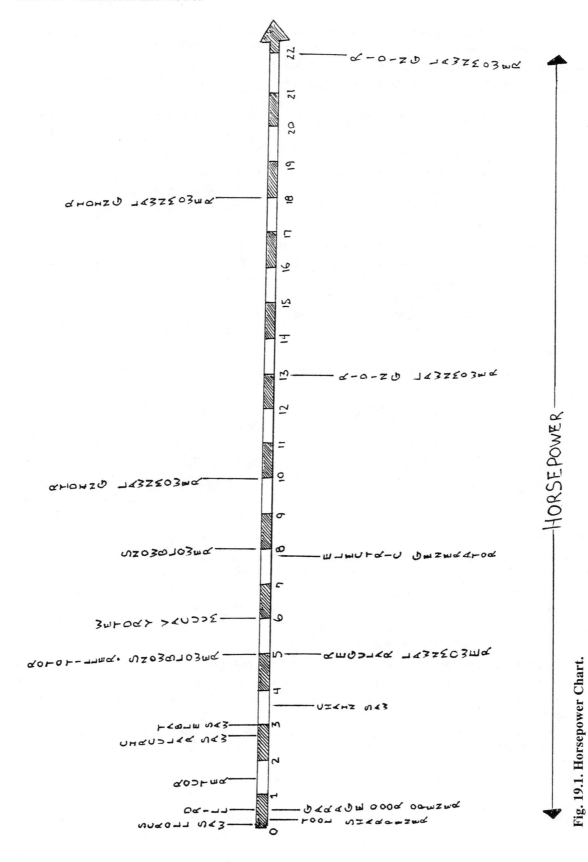

Fig. 19.1. Horsepower Chart.

From *More Science Through Children's Literature.* © 1998 Butzow and Butzow. Teacher Ideas Press. (800) 237-6124.

11. To help children learn more about what makes trucks powerful, invite to class a parent who drives a large commercial truck of any kind. Have children ask the guest questions, such as: How many gears, forward and reverse, does the truck have? What gears are used when driving uphill? Downhill? On a level road? How is a diesel engine different from a standard automobile engine? What are air brakes and why do trucks have them? NOTE: An alternate speaker might be a parent who sells or races bicycles. Ask children how the above questions about trucks relate to bicycles.

12. In the fall, have children take photographs of various sites around the school and in the schoolyard. Have children rephotograph these sites after a snowstorm. What differences do they see? How does snow affect our lives? Have children try drawing the comparison between the fall and winter photographs.

13. Signs in nature can help us to predict snowy weather. Ask children what signs tell people that snow is coming. What are the signs of clearing weather? How do people prepare for winter? For a coming storm?

14. Snow does not accumulate evenly as it covers an area with variable terrain, such as a schoolyard. Have children choose several sites in the schoolyard where snow is likely to accumulate unevenly (e.g., under the swings, beside the school building). After each snowstorm, have children measure the depth of the snow at these sites. Have children calculate the average amount of snow for the playground. NOTE: If children are too young to understand the concept of an average, have them take their measurements using cash register tape. Tape together all the pieces for one site. Divide this cumulative tape into X pieces of equal length, where X is the number of measurements taken at the site. The length of the pieces is the average amount of snowfall at that site. For example, the cash register tapes for one site are 13 inches, 6 inches, 9 inches, and 4 inches. Taped together, they equal 32 inches. Divide this large piece into four pieces. Each piece of paper will equal one-fourth of 32 inches, or 8 inches, which is the average snowfall at that site. Or, have children find the median snowfall for a site: Rank the measurements in order (smallest number to largest number). If there are an odd number of measurements, the median is the middle number; if there are an even number of measurements, the median is the average of the two middle numbers. (Calculating median snowfall will be easier if children take an odd number of measurements.)

15. Have children imagine that a bad winter storm has left their house with no electricity for 24 hours. How would their life change? What would they need to survive? What things would they do differently? Have children write a story about how their life would change and what they would do. NOTE: Have children assume that school has been canceled because of the storm.

16. Have children imagine that a baby has been born at home during a bad snowstorm. The baby and mother will be taken to the hospital on a snowmobile. How would children insulate and protect the baby for this journey?

17. Invite a public safety person to visit the class and talk about the emergency number 911. Allow everyone a chance to practice dialing on a toy phone. Have children practice telling the "operator" their home address and how to get there. Many young children have helped save family lives in this way. NOTE: Children might practice getting emergency help to their home by providing additional information, such as, "it's near the high school," "it's the last house on Warren Road," "it's next to K-Mart."

18. A compass rose is shown on several pages of *Katy and the Big Snow*. In this book, the compass rose does not point to the north, as is typically the case. Have children learn to find directions when north is not designated: Find north in the classroom, then find south, east, and west. Take a walk around the schoolyard to practice finding directions.

19. What is the snowiest month of the winter in your area? Have children keep track of each snowfall and make a bar graph or line graph for each month to represent these numbers (see fig. 19.2). Have children make an accompanying temperature graph for each month (see fig. 19.3). What is the relationship of snowfall to temperature? What other relationships can children deduce? Can they graph these relationships? NOTE: If you do not live in an area with snowy winters, have children "adopt" a city where there is significant snow. A newspaper subscription from that city for a month will provide enough information for children to complete their graphs.

20. Have children pretend that they are the snowplow operator for Katy. Tell children that, because of the snowstorm, they and Katy are the only two "people" who are awake and ready to work in Geoppolis. What does this world look like? How does it feel to see nothing but snow? How does it feel to know that no one will be able to go to work or to school until the roads are clear? After their long, hard—but rewarding—day as a snowplow operator, have children write a letter to their "cousin" in Florida, who never sees snow. They should include in the letter some of their thoughts and feelings about the day's experiences.

21. Have children simulate being caught in the middle of a snowstorm by playing Snow Traveler. Photocopy figures 19.4a and 19.4b, the game board, and figures 19.4c–19.4f, the playing cards. Assemble the board by taping together the two pieces. Cut out the game cards and place them face down at the center of the board. Two to six players can play the game. Each player throws a die once to determine their destination—1 is the hospital, 2 is the drugstore, 3 is the grocery store, 4 is the police station, 5 is the town garage, and 6 is the airport. The object of the game is to be the first player to reach their destination. Each player will need a marker to indicate their position on the board. When a player lands on a snowflake, they draw a card and follow its directions. Cards that have been used are placed face down at the bottom of the stack. Players may choose to move around the board to their destination in either of two possible directions—clockwise or counterclockwise—depending on the shortest route.

Text continues on page 197.

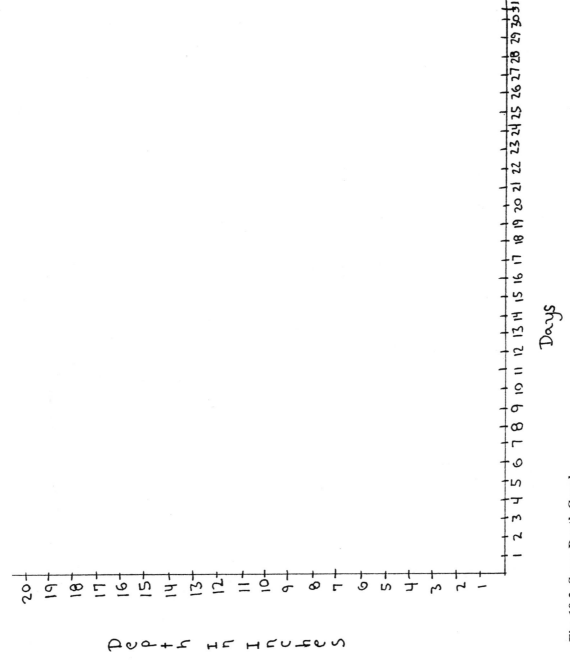

Fig. 19.2. Snow Depth Graph.

From *More Science Through Children's Literature.* © 1998 Butzow and Butzow. Teacher Ideas Press. (800) 237-6124.

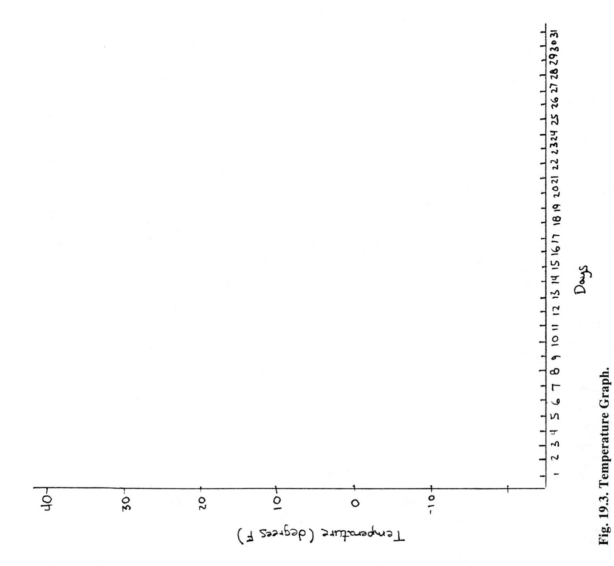

Fig. 19.3. Temperature Graph.

From *More Science Through Children's Literature.* © 1998 Butzow and Butzow. Teacher Ideas Press. (800)

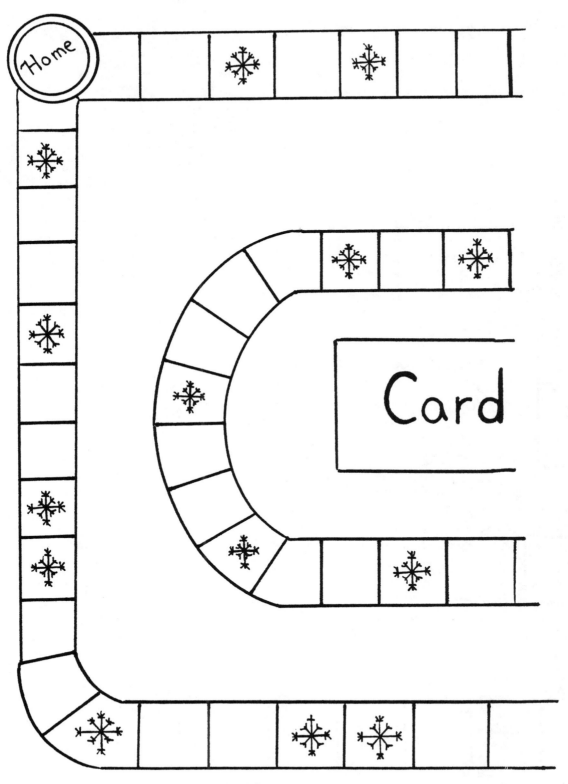

Fig. 19.4a. "Snow Traveler" Game Board.

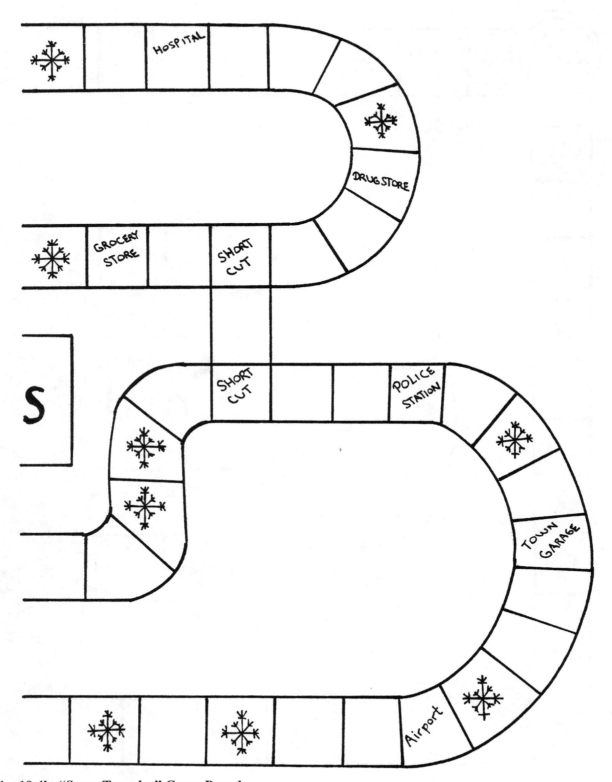

Fig. 19.4b. "Snow Traveler" Game Board.

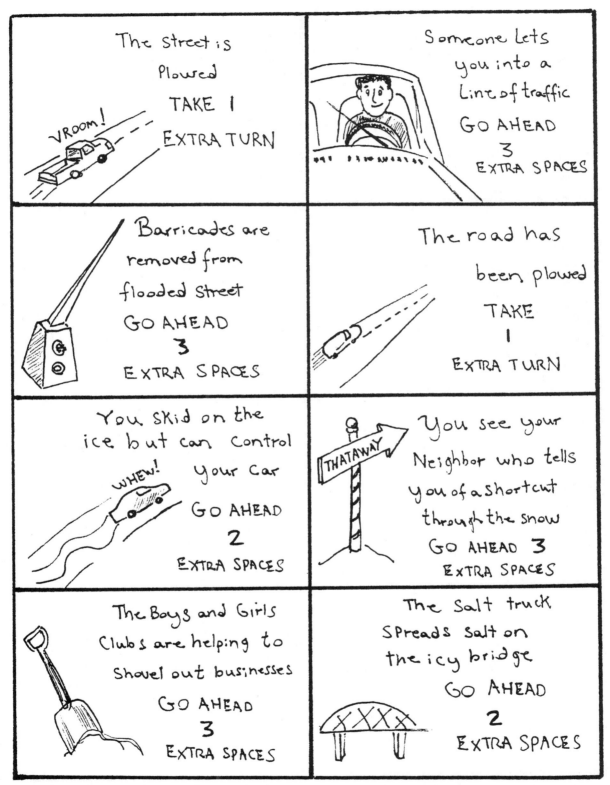

Fig. 19.4c. "Snow Traveler" Playing Cards.

From *More Science Through Children's Literature.* © 1998 Butzow and Butzow. Teacher Ideas Press. (800) 237-6124.

Fig. 19.4d. "Snow Traveler" Playing Cards.

Fig. 19.4e. "Snow Traveler" Playing Cards.

From *More Science Through Children's Literature.* © 1998 Butzow and Butzow. Teacher Ideas Press. (800) 237-6124.

Fig. 19.4f. "Snow Traveler" Playing Cards.

Related Books and References

Burton, Virginia Lee. *Choo Choo*. Boston: Houghton Mifflin, 1937.

———. *The Little House*. Boston: Houghton Mifflin, 1942.

———. *Mike Mulligan and His Steam Shovel*. Boston: Houghton Mifflin, 1930.

Chapter 20

Kites, Wind, and Flight

The Sea-Breeze Hotel

by Marcia Vaughan and Patricia Mullins
New York: Willa Perlman Books (HarperCollins), 1992

Summary

It was too windy at the Sea-Breeze Hotel to swim, to fish, or even to beachcomb. When Sam decided to fly a kite in the wind, wonderful things began to happen, and there were kites everywhere. Tourists filled the Sea-Breeze Hotel to fly kites all year, except April, when the hotel was closed and Sam, his grandpa, Mrs. Pearson, and Hilda went swimming, fishing, and even beachcombing.

Science and Content Related Concepts

Flight, kite flying, kinds of kites, weather, airfoils, Bernoulli's principle

Content Related Words

Air stream, air foil, air pressure, boisterous, blustery, buffeting, beachcombing, anemometer

Activities

1. Kites have long been used for scientific and religious purposes, as well as for recreation. In the library media center or at a local library, have children locate books about the history and use of kites. Have children make a related timeline that includes the work of the following people: Archytas of Tarentum, Alexander Wilson, Thomas Melville, Ben Franklin, William Eddy, Lawrence Hargrave, Alexander Graham Bell, and the Wright brothers. Children should include the contributions of each person to the art or science of kite flying. Other information related to the history of kites might be added to the timeline as well.

2. A spring balance measures force. Have children attach a spring balance to the string of a flying kite (see fig. 20.1). Have them determine how hard the kite pulls on the string. Compare the force readings on the spring balance for several kinds of kites flying under the same wind conditions. Does one kind of kite exert more of a force (i.e., have more lift) than other kinds of kites? NOTE: The most common kites include bow kite, flat kite, and box kite.

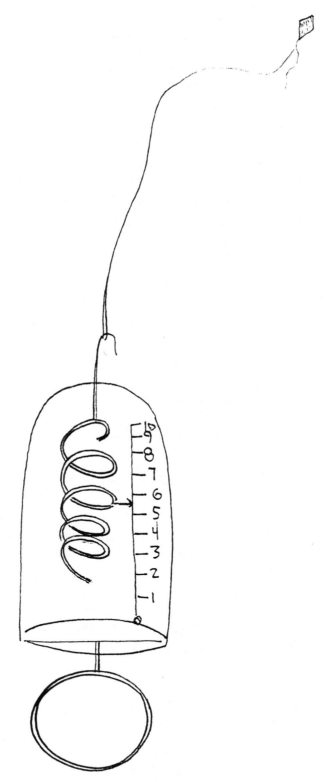

Fig. 20.1. Measuring the Force (Lift) of a Kite.

From *More Science Through Children's Literature.* © 1998 Butzow and Butzow. Teacher Ideas Press. (800) 237-6124.

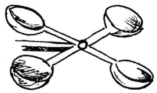

Fig. 20.2. Anemometer.

3. Using an anemometer (see fig. 20.2) to measure the wind speed, have children compare the abilities of various kinds of kites to remain aloft as wind speed changes. Do kites with particular shapes fly better when the wind speed is low? Do particular kinds of kites need a stronger wind to attain flight and remain aloft?

4. Ask a library media specialist to help children find books about kites and kite flying. Have children draw pictures of the various kinds of kites. How did the use of kites lead to the invention of the airplane? How was the invention of the glider instrumental in the invention of the airplane?

5. Have children learn how kites were used in other cultures, historically, especially in the Orient. What were kites used for in the United States (e.g., as a means of gathering weather data)? How and why are kites still used today in this country?

6. Have children make a kite following these directions:

   a. Open out a 16-by-24-inch piece of newspaper and draw a diamond kite shape on it (see fig. 20.3).

   b. Cut two thin dowels to fit across the diamond (one crosswise, one lengthwise). Tie the dowels together where they cross at the center of the kite.

   c. Tie string around the perimeter of the cross, tying the string firmly to the end of each dowel. (Tie the string about one inch from the edge of the dowels, to allow an overlap of paper for step e.)

   d. Lay the kite frame on the newspaper diamond. Fold the edges of the paper over the string and glue them to the kite's body.

   e. Punch two holes in the kite, as shown in figure 20.3, and tie a piece of string to the crosswise dowel.

   f. Tie a kite string to the front of the kite (tie it to the string added in step e), and tie a tail onto the kite. NOTE: A tail consists of a knotted piece of old cloth, about as long as the kite itself. The tail keeps the kite steady so that it always flies in the same direction. As preparation for flying kites, have children do the following:

      • Enlist the aid of a parent or other person who has experience in flying kites. Together, make a list of steps that one should follow in launching and sailing a kite, including making a tail for the kite and the position one uses to hold the kite as it is launched.

      • With the volunteer who will help launch the kites, make a list of safety rules for flying kites (e.g., do not fly a kite near power lines).

      • Determine the best weather for flying kites. What kinds of clouds indicate weather that is breezy, yet manageable and favorable for flying kites? What land features indicate an area well suited for flying kites? How much space will be necessary to fly kites, assuming that several will be launched at the same time? Do certain kites fly best in a particular type of wind (e.g., a strong wind, a gusty wind, a gentle breeze)? Check the weather conditions for the day you want to launch a kite. This may help you determine the best time for flying a kite. Those who have experience flying kites can help you choose the best day and locale for flying a kite.

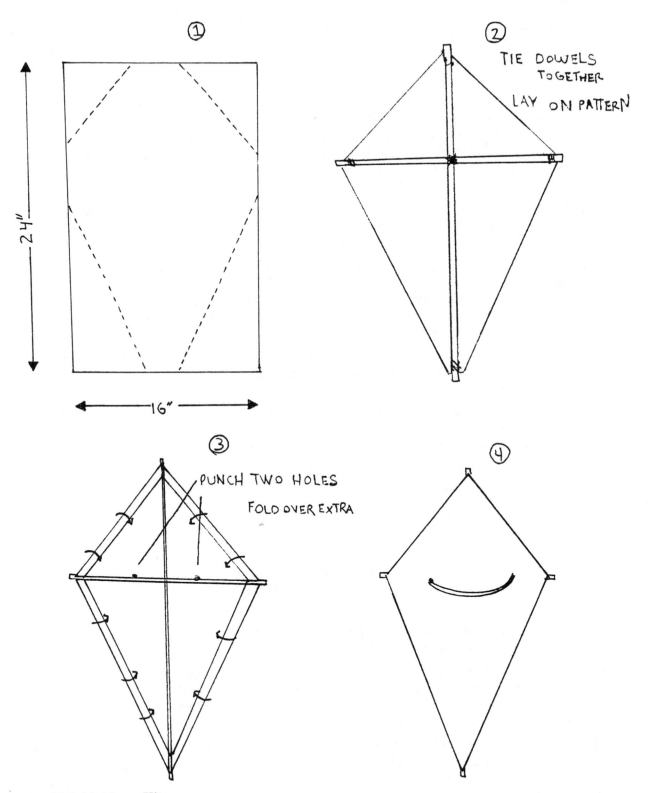

Fig. 20.3. Making a Kite.

From *More Science Through Children's Literature.* © 1998 Butzow and Butzow. Teacher Ideas Press. (800) 237-6124.

7. Ask children how the flight of an airplane is similar to the flight of a kite. Have children compare the four forces acting upon an airplane—lift, gravity, thrust, and drag—with the forces acting upon a kite in flight. (See Chapter 21, "Airplanes and Flight"—activity 5 in particular—for more information about airplane flight.)

8. An air foil is the surface against which the wind blows. Examples of air foils include airplane wings, sails on sailboats, kites, airplane propellers, blades of fans, and spoilers on automobiles. Ask children if they can, using their knowledge of kites (and airplanes— see Chapter 21, "Airplanes and Flight"), explain how an air foil works. What purpose does an air foil serve? How would increasing or decreasing the size of an air foil change its performance?

9. In addition to constructing a working kite, have children make miniature kites of various kinds (e.g., bow kites, box kites, and flat kites—see fig. 20.4). Have children display their miniature kites on a bulletin board or as a wall mural for others in the school to see.

10. The illustrations in *The Sea-Breeze Hotel* include various art forms and may help children use art techniques that are new to them (e.g., torn-tissue collage; use of fabrics, feathers, and string; sketches). Point out to children how various techniques are combined in the illustrations to produce art that is pleasing to the eye. Have children try some of these techniques. Display their art on the bulletin board or in the wall mural (see activity 9).

11. *The Sea-Breeze Hotel* describes the winds as being "boisterous, blustery, and buffeting." This technique, repetition of an initial sound in neighboring words, is called alliteration. Have children select letters or sounds and write alliterative verses with them.

12. Haiku is an unrhymed form of Japanese poetry. Have children compose haiku poetry, using kites or flying as the subject. The haiku poem, which typically celebrates nature using metaphor, contains three lines:

    Line 1—5 syllables

    Line 2—7 syllables

    Line 3—5 syllables

Example

The wind is blowing
My kite is flying above
Kites embrace the breeze

Children might write their haiku poetry on their miniature kites made in activity 9 or on their kite timelines made in activity 1.

13. Have children tape together two sheets of blue 8½-by-11-inch construction paper along the widthwise edges to make an 8½-by-22-inch sheet of paper. Have children make several kites to fly in this blue sky. This project will probably fit on a locker door or in any narrow spot on a wall in the classroom.

14. Have children pretend that their aunt and uncle own the Sea-Breeze Hotel. Tell children that their aunt and uncle will hire them if they can help bring customers to the hotel by writing an attractive brochure. Children should include reasons why tourists should spend their vacation at the Sea-Breeze Hotel.

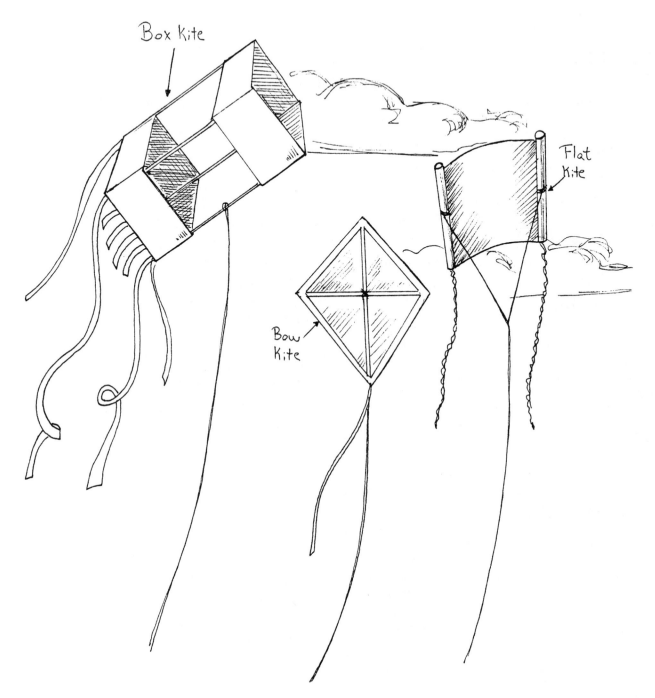

Fig. 20.4. Kinds of Kites.

15. Crossword—Kite Flying

CLUES

Across

2. Kites are often made in the form of this fierce creature

4. Kite with tension on one of the crosspieces

5. Stay away from electrical _____ when flying a kite

7. Keeps the kite connected to the person who flies the kite

8. Brothers who experimented with kites before they invented the airplane

10. Pyramid-shaped kite perfected by the man who invented the telephone

13. In Asian countries, kite flying was often a part of the _____ of the people

14. Helps give a kite its stability

16. Kite Day is celebrated on the ninth day of the ninth month in this country

17. Keeps the kite up in the air

Down

1. Square-shaped kite invented by Hargrave in Australia

3. *The Sea-Breeze Hotel* takes place in this country

4. Kites are often made in the form of this insect

6. Kites are often flown to _____ oneself, to have fun

9. American who flew a kite to learn more about electricity

11. Also known as a "plain" kite, it must have a tail to fly

12. Usually an excellent month for flying kites

15. Asian country known for its delicate kites

16. Kites were used to _____ objects

WORDS USED

Australia	entertain	string
bow	flat	tail
box	Franklin	tetrahedral
butterfly	Japan	wind
carry	March	wires
China	religion	Wright
dragon		

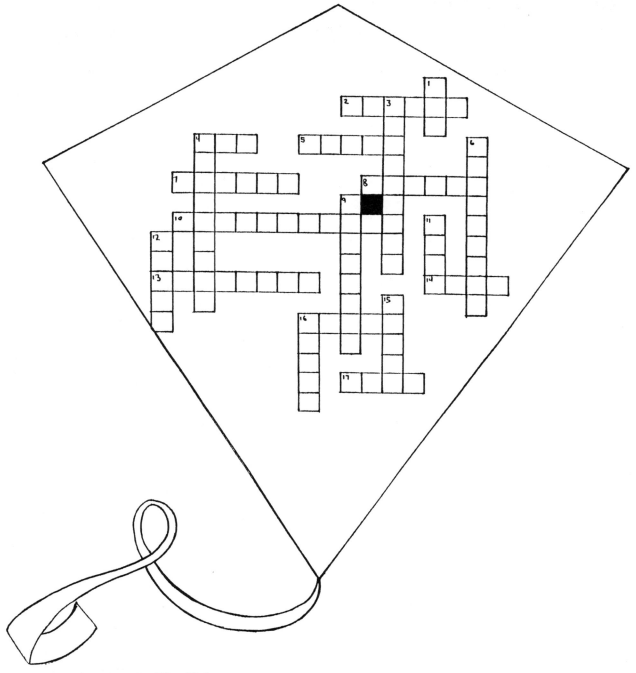

Fig. 20.5. Crossword—Kite Flying.

Related Books and References

Hardy, Garry, and Marvin N. Tolman. "Pencil Point Anemometer." *Science and Children* 33, no. 7 (April 1996): 10.

Lloyd, Ambrose, and Nicolette Thomas. *Kites and Kite Flying*. New York: Hamlyn, 1978.

Chapter 21

Airplanes and Flight

Plane Song

by Diane Siebert
New York: HarperCollins, 1993

Summary

This book of narrative poetry tells the story of modern aviation. It explains the various kinds of aircraft and the many purposes that they serve.

Science and Content Related Concepts

Principles of flight, kinds of aircraft, careers in aviation, Bernoulli's principle

Content Related Words

Airport, runway, cargo, bomber, Mach

Activities

1. Before beginning this unit, write to the National Coalition for Aviation Education for a catalog titled "A Guide to Aviation Education Resources," which is published by the Federal Aviation Administration and the Department of Transportation. Free materials on aviation education can be ordered through this clearinghouse. Allow several weeks to receive the catalog. Sample organizations that have aviation education materials to offer include the General Aviation Manufacturers Association (phone 202-393-1500) and the Aircraft Owners and Pilots Association (phone 301-695-2000).

   National Coalition for Aviation Education
   P.O. Box 28068
   Washington, DC 20038
   (718) 553-3363

2. Use *Plane Song* as a choral reading selection. Divide the piece into sections and distribute them to small groups, large groups, and individuals. Children should be allowed ample time to practice their parts before "performing" the piece. Pantomimes or dance might be included in the presentation. NOTE: Check with school officials on the legalities of reproducing copyrighted material.

3. One of the most important things to understand in the study of aviation is the role that air plays in the flying of the plane. Have children perform the following experiments to understand more about air:

a. Air occupies space.

Inflate a balloon. Children can see how much space the air occupies by how large the balloon becomes.

Stuff a tissue into a small, plastic cup. Invert the cup and place it levelly into a bowl of water (see fig. 21.1). Submerge the cup to just past the level of the tissue. Remove the cup and verify that the tissue was protected by the air in the cup and has remained dry.

Fig. 21.1. Trapping Air in a Cup.

b. Air has weight.

On an arm balance, place an empty balloon on one side of the balance and an inflated balloon on the other (see fig. 21.2). Which balloon has more weight? How can children account for this?

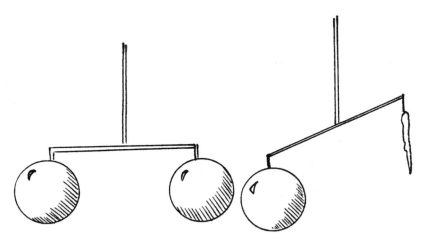

Fig. 21.2. Weighing Air Using Balloons.

c. Air exerts pressure.

Completely fill a small glass with water. Cover it with a piece of thin cardboard, which is about four inches square. Invert the glass, holding the card in place. Gently take your hand off the card. Air pressure will force the card to stay in place.

Fill a medicine dropper (or kitchen baster) with water from a small container (see fig. 21.3). Lift the dropper out of the water. The water will not run out because the air pressure forces it to stay inside the tube.

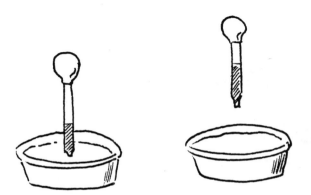

Fig. 21.3. Air Pressure Holding Liquid in a Medicine Dropper.

d. Air moves.

Notice how tree leaves move or how smoke from a fire twists and turns as it rises. This is caused by air moving. By observation, how else can children prove that air moves?

Make a simple pinwheel. Cut out the pinwheel pattern in figure 21.4; cut along the diagonal lines of the pattern. Bring together the four labeled points so that they overlap at the center of the pinwheel. Push a pin through the centered points, then through the center of the pinwheel. Push the pin into the eraser of a pencil. Blow air onto the pinwheel outside and notice how the air moves the blades of the pinwheel.

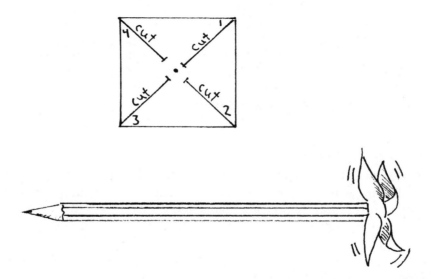

Fig. 21.4. Making a Pinwheel.

e. Air expands when heated, contracts when cooled.

Partially inflate a balloon. Hold the balloon near a source of heat, such as a hot-air heat register or vent (see fig. 21.5). Heat will cause the air to expand. Ask children whether this will happen if they put the balloon into a dish of hot water. NOTE: The balloon will again increase in size. Blow soap bubbles. As the air in the bubbles cools, they will contract.

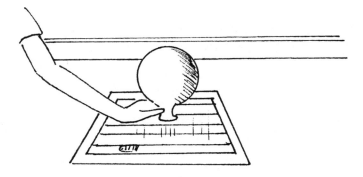

Fig. 21.5. Heated Air Expands.

f.   Air contains moisture.

Fill a glass with ice water. Over time, water vapor in the air will condense onto the outside of the glass as water (see fig. 21.6). If the temperature of the glass is low enough, the water that condenses will quickly freeze.

Fig. 21.6. Moisture in Air.

g. Air provides resistance.

Think of the many things that are held up by air (e.g., tree seeds, paper airplanes, parachutes, birds, bats, kites, gliders, airplanes). Make and fly a paper helicopter (see fig. 21.7). How can the paper helicopter be modified to stay in the air longer?

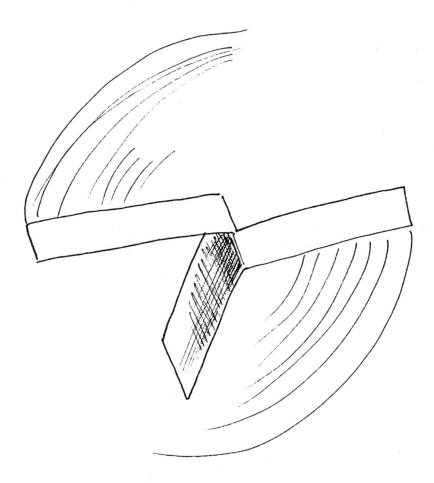

Fig. 21.7. Paper Helicopter.

4. The force that causes a plane to rise is called lift. Children can see this force at work by performing an experiment that demonstrates Bernoulli's principle: Hold a sheet of paper between thumb and forefinger on both sides. Let both sides of the paper droop. Put the paper near the lips and blow across the curve. As you do this, the free end of the paper will rise slightly. For the airplane wing (see fig. 21.8), faster-moving air blows across the top of the wing and causes the air pressure on top of the wing to decrease. The slower-moving air beneath the wing increases the pressure on the underside of the wing. This combination of decreased and increased pressure helps lift the airplane off the ground.

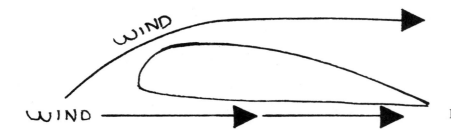

Fig. 21.8. Wing and Airflow.

5. Explain to children the four forces that act upon an airplane in flight (see fig. 21.9):

   a. Lift is the force that causes the plane to rise.

   b. Gravity is the force that causes the plane to descend.

   c. Thrust is the force that propels the plane forward.

   d. Drag is the force that slows the forward movement of the plane.

   How can children explain the effects of these four forces as an airplane is taking off? Are similar forces at work upon human beings as they perform various actions?

6. One of the many things that a pilot must know is the direction in which they are flying. The four basic directions are north, south, east, and west. By subdividing the basic directional compass into smaller parts, northeast, southeast, southwest, and northwest are defined. You may wish to have children look at the compass on fig. 17.1 on p. 165. Have the children show that they understand these eight basic directions by associating them with objects in the classroom.

7. To practice using directions, have children stand facing north. Tell them that east is to their right; south is to their back; and west is to their left, and that northeast is midway between north and east; northwest is midway between north and west; and so forth. To increase children's familiarity with these compass points, play a game of Simon Says (i.e., "Simon Says, 'Go north' "; "Simon says, 'Go southeast' "; etc.). When the statement is said without the phrase "Simon Says" as part of the direction, children do not do what is asked of them; they must sit down if they have done so. NOTE: Until children are able to think abstractly about which direction they are facing, have them reorient themselves (turn back to north) at the beginning of each turn.

8. Once children have mastered directions, have them use a circle protractor to learn the degree designations associated with directions: North is 0 degrees (or 360 degrees); east is 90 degrees; south is 180 degrees; and west is 270 degrees. Have children practice identifying the directions by degrees. Then, use math problems to help children become more proficient (e.g., If you turn from east to north, clockwise, how many degrees have you turned? If you are moving west and turn 270 degrees, in what direction are you headed? If you are moving south, what direction is 45 degrees to you right?).

9. A field trip to an airport can help children learn more about airplanes. Contact a local airport to arrange a tour. Before the trip, have children brainstorm questions that they would like to have answered when they visit. NOTE: Visiting a small airport may be more rewarding for children than visiting a large airport because they can often see the planes at closer range, and may be allowed to sit in a cockpit.

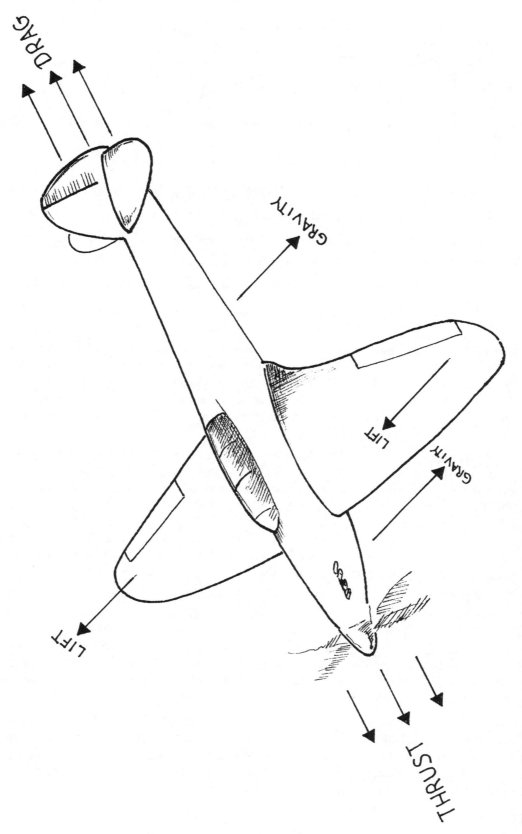

Fig. 21.9. The Four Forces Acting upon an Airplane in Flight.

From *More Science Through Children's Literature.* © 1998 Butzow and Butzow. Teacher Ideas Press. (800) 237-6124.

10. Many parts of the airport, itself, are important for children to see and understand. During a guided tour, children will probably visit these areas: reception desk, weather station, maintenance shop, flight school, traffic control area, arrival and departure gates, waiting area, pilot's lounge, ticketing desk, fueling station, security areas, and airplane hangers. Have children learn the purposes of each of these areas.

11. Airports are often divided into three sections—general aviation, commercial flights, and military aircraft. Have children visit these areas (if present) during their visit and compare how they are alike and different. Which types of aircraft are found in each of these areas? (e.g., 737s and 747s are commercial planes; planes made by the Beechcraft Company are usually used for general aviation).

12. Have children write thank-you letters to the persons who guided their tour of the airport. Children might want to include drawings related to the field trip.

13. If it is not possible to visit an airport, invite airport personnel to visit the class. Such personnel might include pilots, but airports employ people of many other professions, all of whom can educate children about some aspect of an airport.

14. One of the many important duties of a pilot is to file a flight plan for each trip they take. This plan includes the destination of the flight, as well as information about the route and how long it will take to reach the destination. Have children practice making flight plans using a road map. Select a town about 100 miles away. Plan which highways will be used and list the towns that will be passed through. Assuming a traveling speed of approximately 50 miles per hour, how long will it take to complete the journey? NOTE: Remind children that pilots do not use road maps; nor do they follow highways. Using road maps is but a first step in teaching navigation. Local politicians and transportation departments can supply (or recommend sources for) state road maps.

15. Have children pretend that they are the pilot of a plane. Using a road map, lay a ruler from your city or town to a destination (because flight is, generally, in a straight line). Over which towns will children fly? Have children lay a circle protractor on the map and take a bearing to determine in which direction they are traveling. Assuming a traveling speed of approximately 100 miles per hour, how long will it take to complete the journey?

16. *Plane Song* shows that an airplane has many uses. For example, planes can be used for carrying passengers, transporting cargo, or various military purposes. They can also be used for fighting fires, predicting weather, dusting crops, mail service, medical transport, or pleasure. Ask children if they can think of any other ways in which airplanes are used. Have children select the type of airplane of which they would most like to be a pilot. Have them write a description of their life as that pilot, including a self-portrait in their uniform.

17. To encourage children to study the careers in aviation, bring to class hats that represent the different facets of aviation. Include hats that represent the occupations on and off the ground that children learned about during this unit or while visiting an airport.

18. Have children search the Internet using the word *airplane*. Making paper airplanes can enhance children's study of aviation. Two Web sites in particular that will supply children with information about making paper airplanes are http://pchelp.inc.net/paperairplanes/plane-5.html and http://www.dsw.com/templt.html.

19. Have children make a paper airplane following figure 21.10. Can they modify the design to make the plane fly higher or faster?

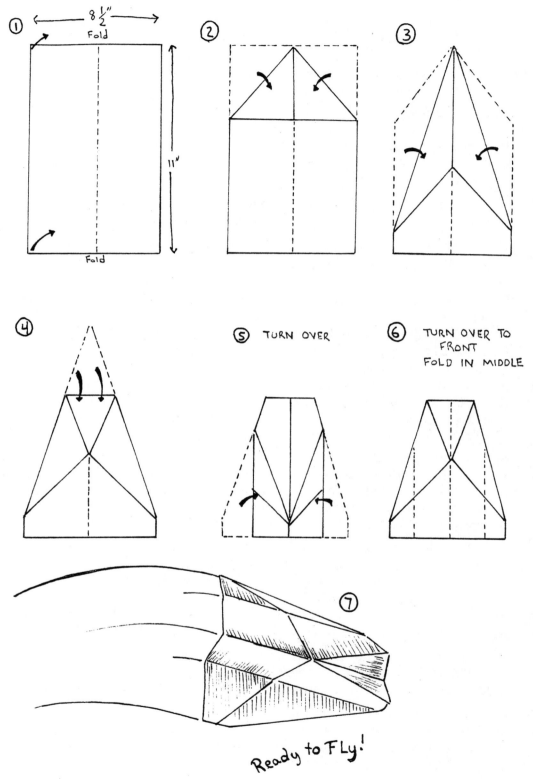

Fig. 21.10. Making a Paper Airplane.

20. *The Paper Airplane Book* by Seymour Simon is an engaging good source of information about making paper airplanes. Have students try to fold and fly some of Mr. Simon's planes.

21. Children can learn about the early pioneers of aviation by reading *The Big Balloon Race* by Eleanor Coerr and *The Glorious Flight* by Martin Provensen and Alice Provensen. Check the library media center for other information on the history of flight.

22. Word Search—Airplanes

   Words related to airplanes are hidden in this word search—horizontally, vertically, and diagonally, forwards and backwards. First, match the words to the clues.

CLUES

a. Force that raises a plane

b. Speed of sound

c. Body of an airplane

d. Building to house airplanes

e. Strip of paved land for takeoffs and landings

f. Force of the Earth's pull

g. On the inside of the wing; they help control downward movement

h. One who travels between home and another city to work

i. Mechanical implements for use in poor visibility

j. Moveable control on an airplane wing; used for turning

k. Rear of the plane; includes the rudder

l. Force that slows a body in motion

m. Directed force

n. Rotating blades that pull an aircraft forward

o. Space for the pilot and crew

p. Wheels that touch the ground (two words)

q. Located on the tail; it helps steer the plane

r. Freight carried by an airplane

s. Airplane that does not use a propeller

t. Parts that provide lift and support

u. Place for airplane arrivals and departures

WORDS USED

ailerons	fuselage	Mach
airport	gravity	propeller
cargo	hangar	rudder
cockpit	instruments	runway
commuter	jet	tail
drag	landing gear	thrust
flaps	lift	wings

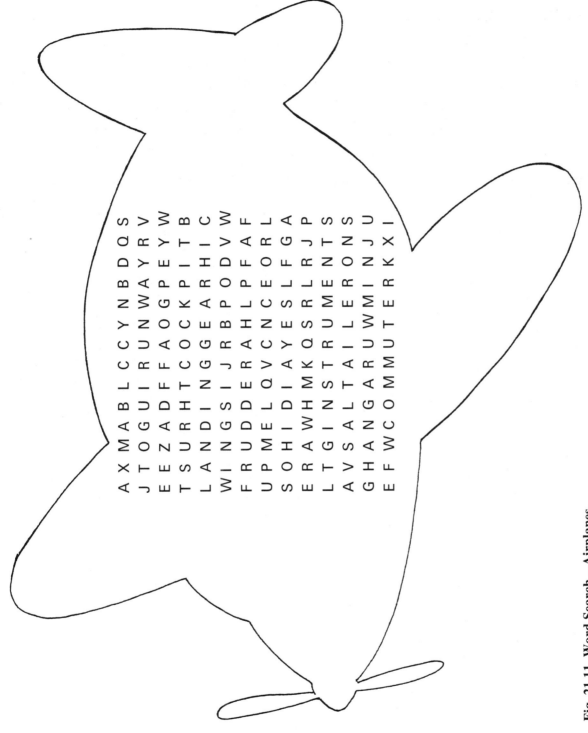

Fig. 21.11. Word Search—Airplanes.

From *More Science Through Children's Literature*. © 1998 Butzow and Butzow. Teacher Ideas Press. (800) 237-6124.

Related Books and References

Baird, Kate A., Louedith Hara, Kristi Perryman-Dyer, and Dolores A. Buckabee. "When Science Soars." *The Science Teacher* 64, no. 2 (February 1997): 30–33.

Coerr, Eleanor. *The Big Balloon Race*. New York: Harper & Row, 1981.

Keeler, Lagneia. "We're Flying Now!" *Science and Children* 31, no. 5 (February 1994): 44.

Provensen, Martin, and Alice Provensen. *The Glorious Flight*. New York: Viking, 1983.

Simon, Seymour. *The Paper Airplane Book*. New York: Viking Press, 1971.

Tamarkin, Cali, and Barbara Bourne. "Soaring with Science." *Science and Children* 33, no. 2 (October 1995): 20–23.

Appendix

Answer Keys

Chapter 1—*Here Is the Arctic Winter*

The answers to the math puzzle are owl, narwhal, caribou, fox, ptarmigan, wolf, hare, cod, bear, and seal.

Chapter 2—*Winter Whale*

WORD SEARCH ANSWERS —WHALING

a.	Towards the back of the boat	aft
b.	Heavy piece of iron used to hold a boat in place	anchor
c.	It strains plankton from the seawater	baleen
d.	Containers for oil	barrels
e.	Thick layer of fat between the whale's skin and muscle	blubber
f.	Forward part of the boat	bow
g.	Small, flat-bottomed boat	dory
h.	Tail of the whale	flukes
i.	"All hands on _____!"	deck
j.	Towards the front of the boat	fore
k.	Ship's kitchen	galley
l.	Spearlike instrument for fastening onto a whale	harpoon
m.	Warm-blooded animal that nurses its young	mammal
n.	Large pole for holding rigging and sails	mast
o.	Boat being towed through the water by a whale	Nantucket Sleigh Ride
p.	To direct the ship's course	navigate
q.	Right side of a sailing vessel	starboard
r.	Left side of a sailing vessel	port
s.	Sailing vessel with two or more masts	schooner
t.	Officer in charge of a vessel	captain
u.	Top of the whale's head	blowhole
v.	Rear end of a vessel	stern
w.	It was burned for lighting purposes	oil
x.	To measure the depth of water	sound
y.	Group or gathering of whales	pod
z.	From here came cries of "Land ahoy!"	crow's nest

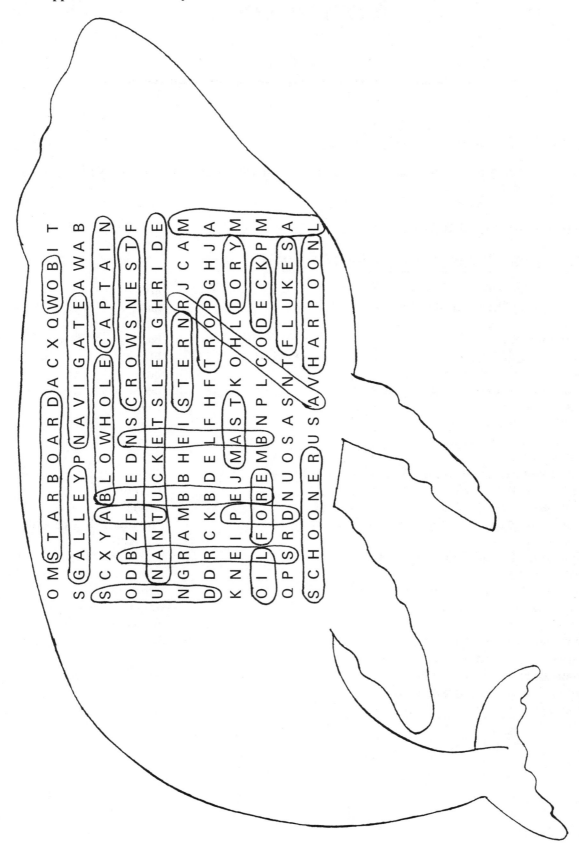

Fig. 2.4. Word Search—Whaling.

Chapter 3—*One Small Fish*

CROSSWORD ANSWERS—FRESHWATER AQUARIUM

Across

1. Fish with a large tail	guppy
4. Where fish live in the classroom	aquarium
5. Fish with a bright line down its side	neon
9. Fish that lives on the bottom of the aquarium	catfish
10. Creature that creeps along the side of the aquarium	snail

Down

2. Something green that grows in the aquarium	plant
3. It pushes air into the aquarium	pump
4. Fish with stripes down its body (two words)	angel fish
6. Fish swim and thrive in this liquid	water
7. Rocks at the bottom of the aquarium	gravel
8. Removes impurities from the water	filter

CROSSWORD ANSWERS—SALTWATER AQUARIUM

Across

4. It sounds more like a vegetable (two words)	sea cucumber
7. You can't "spend" this creature (two words)	sand dollar
8. Small inhabitants of the intertidal zone	fish

Down

1. Critter with two shells that hangs onto rocks with a beardlike substance	mussel
2. Its "heavenly" shape is made up of five arms	starfish
3. Animal with 10 appendages that walks sideways	crab
5. "Slow as a _____ ."	snail
6. Animal that moves by means of a large foot, which comes out from between its two shells	clam

Fig. 3.6. Crossword—Freshwater Aquarium.

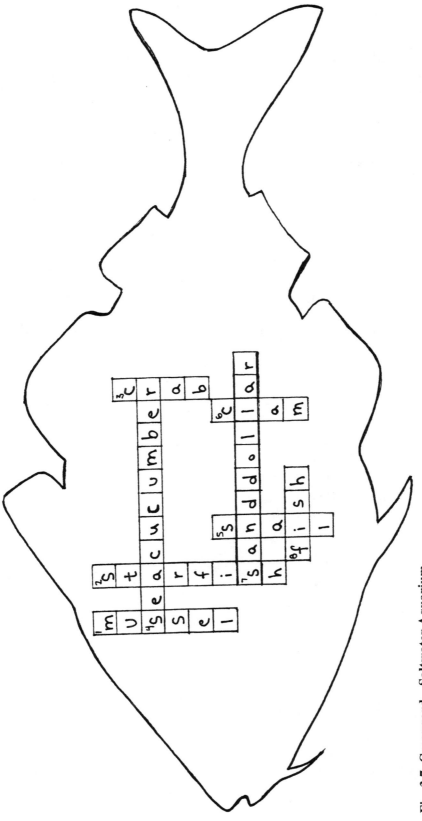

Fig. 3.7. Crossword—Saltwater Aquarium.

Chapter 4—*One Morning in Maine*

WORD LADDER ANSWERS—SEAWEED

1. I attach myself to _____ so that I can stay in one spot.   rocks
2. I am a small, bubblelike part of seaweed that enables it   float
   to _____ in the water.
3. I am a green pigment in plants. I am called _____ .   chlorophyll
4. I am a common color for seaweed. I am _____ .   green
5. I am a member of a large group of water plants known   algae
   as _____ .
6. I am a tough leathery seaweed called _____   Irish moss
   _____ . I am important as a source of agar.
7. I am a plant that lives in ocean waters. I can be green, red, or   seaweed
   brown. I am _____ .
8. I am given off by seaweed and help keep the water pure. I   oxygen
   am _____ .
9. I am the great brown algae of northern waters known   kelps
   as _____ .
10. I am rich in potash, so I can be used in the manufacture   fertilizer
    of _____ .
11. I am a thickening agent used in the preparation of soup. I   agar
    am _____ .

```
            ROCKS
             FLOAT
        CHLOROPHYLL
              GREEN
              ALGAE
            IRISH  MOSS
              SEAWEED
              OXYGEN

        KELPS
            FERTILIZER
              AGAR
```

Chapter 5—*Stellaluna*

WORD LADDER ANSWERS—BATS

1. Bat droppings   guano
2. Sensing device that helps locate prey   echolocation
3. Dense tropical forest (two words)   rain forest
4. Species of bats that suck blood (two words)   vampire bats
5. Species of bats known by their color (two words)   red bats
6. To take pollen from one plant to another   pollination

7. Science of raising crops — agriculture
8. Bugs that bats eat — insects
9. To sleep through the winter — hibernation
10. To break up and scatter — disperse
11. Having to do with nighttime — noctural
12. Animal that preys on another animal — predator
13. Ecological community — ecosystem
14. Mistaken or wrong idea — misconception
15. Desert plant pollinated by bats — cactus
16. Warm-blooded animals — mammals
17. Natural environment where an animal lives — habitat

<u>E</u>CHOLOCATION
POLLI<u>N</u>ATION
PRE<u>D</u>ATOR
M<u>A</u>MMALS
NOCTUR<u>N</u>AL
<u>G</u>UANO
<u>E</u>COSYSTEM
<u>R</u>AIN FOREST
AGRICULTUR<u>E</u>
<u>D</u>ISPERSE

CACTU<u>S</u>
MISCONCE<u>P</u>TION
VAMPIR<u>E</u> BATS
INSE<u>C</u>TS
HAB<u>I</u>TAT
HIB<u>E</u>RNATION
RED BAT<u>S</u>

Chapter 7—*Cactus Hotel*

WORD SCRAMBLE ANSWERS—ANIMALS OF THE ARIZONA DESERT

a. coyote
b. scorpion
c. lizard
d. snake
e. woodpecker
f. ant
g. spider
h. finch
i. squirrel
j. dove
k. hummingbird
l. gila monster
m. fox
n. bat
o. roadrunner
p. mouse
q. owl
r. packrat
s. jackrabbit

Chapter 9—*The Sun, the Wind and the Rain*

WORD SCRAMBLE ANSWERS—GEOLOGY

a. earth
b. mountain
c. rock
d. shift
e. erosion

f. canyons
g. valley
h. plain
i. stratum
j. rain

WORD LADDER ANSWERS—EROSION

1.	Where we live	Earth
2.	It waters the earth	rain
3.	Top layer of land that can be washed away by wind or rain	soil
4.	Final destination of running water	sea
5.	It blows away particles of soil	wind
6.	It freezes in the cracks of the mountain and breaks the rock	snow
7.	Heat from here can crack rocks	Sun

EARTH
RAIN
SOIL
SEA
WIND
SNOW
SUN

Chapter 10—*In Coal Country*

CROSSWORD ANSWERS—*IN COAL COUNTRY*

Across

1.	Mother used this process to preserve food	canning
3.	Specific time when one worked at the mine (3 words)	hoot owl shift
6.	Pile of waste material (two words)	gob pile
7.	Wash boilers were made of this metal	copper
8.	He repaired the railroads (two words)	paddy man
9.	Streets were made of this material (two words)	red dog
10.	Substances dug from the ground	minerals
13.	They carried the coal to Ohio	trains
18.	Pa wore these to protect his feet (three words)	steel-toed shoes

Down

1.	Dug from the ground in the mines	coal
2.	Group of houses in a coal mining village (two words)	company row
4.	Device to wash and sort coal	tipple

5. Pa wore trousers made from this faded cloth — denim
10. Underground area containing coal — mine
11. Pa shelled these for Mother's Christmas cakes — nuts
12. Flowers for Mother's table — violets
14. It signified the end of a shift or work time — whistle
15. Pail to carry a lunch — bucket
16. These animals worked in the mines — mules
17. State near Pennsylvania and West Virginia — Ohio

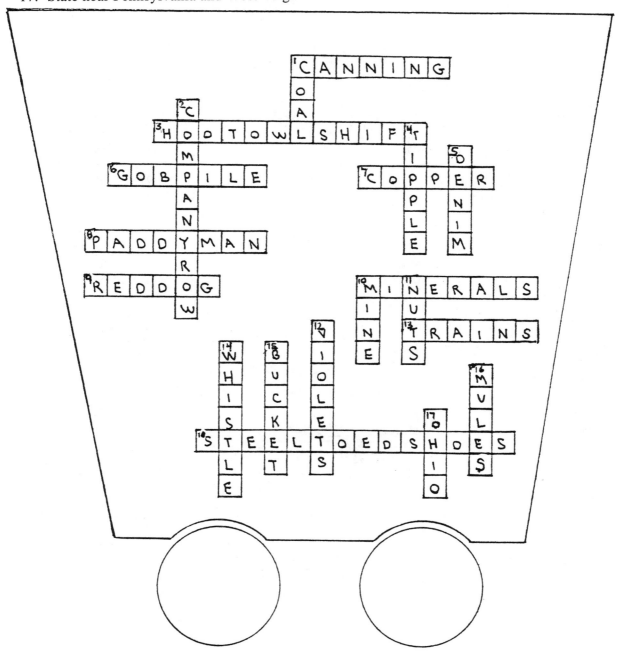

Fig. 10.4. Crossword—*In Coal Country.*

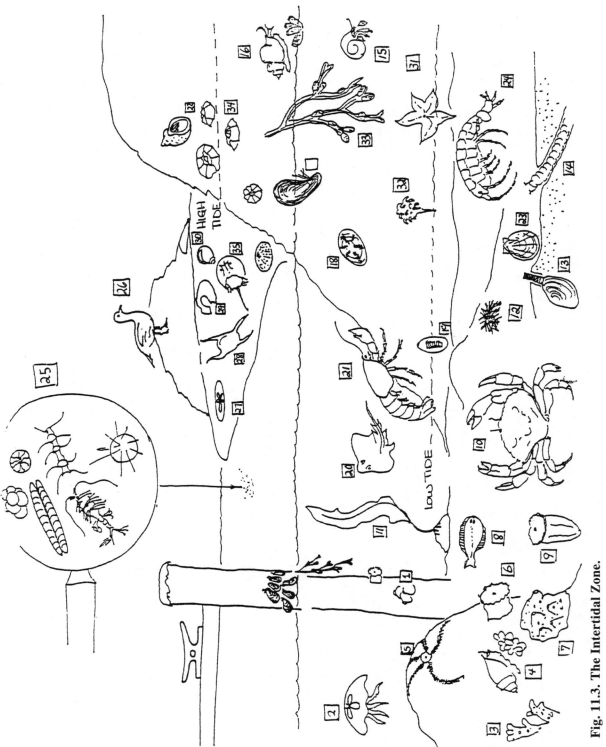

Fig. 11.3. The Intertidal Zone.

Chapter 12—*Sun Up*

WORD SEARCH ANSWERS — *SUN UP*

a.	It accompanied thunder	lightning
b.	It announced that morning had begun	rooster
c.	He was the father's assistant	helper
d.	Young man who went fishing	boy
e.	Bright yellow flower	sunflower
f.	It spun its web in the barn	spider
g.	Sudden rushes of rain, sometimes with thunder and lightning	storms
h.	It tied bundle of food for cows (two words)	hay baler
i.	Place where the animals drank	pond
j.	They swam in the pond	fish
k.	Place where the animals slept	barn
l.	Small, chirping insect	cricket
m.	It could be seen in the sky	catbird
n.	Small rodent	mouse
o.	It flapped its wings in trying to fly	chicken
p.	Kind of tree	sycamore
q.	Swiftly flowing water	stream
r.	Machine that helped the farmer plant and harvest	tractor
s.	Man who owned the farm	farmer
t.	Dark one may indicate a storm	cloud
u.	Place where eggs were gathered	henhouse
v.	They were milked each day	cows
w.	Family's pet	dog

S	U	N	F	L	O	W	E	R	B	O	Y	S
C	A	X	R	E	L	A	B	Y	A	H	W	M
R	Y	T	A	M	O	B	P	H	R	P	R	B
I	Q	R	C	H	I	C	K	E	N	R	T	X
C	S	A	T	A	F	L	B	N	C	O	W	S
K	Y	C	O	C	D	O	G	H	S	I	F	D
E	C	T	I	C	F	U	P	O	N	D	A	Z
T	A	O	M	A	C	D	K	U	C	E	R	V
A	M	R	S	T	O	R	M	S	L	R	M	Z
R	O	E	P	B	W	P	O	E	O	D	E	T
B	R	Q	I	I	G	E	U	L	U	H	R	V
S	E	F	D	R	O	H	S	M	D	C	G	S
F	T	B	E	D	P	H	E	L	P	E	R	L
C	A	H	R	O	O	S	T	E	R	I	K	I
L	I	G	H	T	N	I	N	G	A	J	B	M
D	N	E	H	E	D	F	O	H	S	T	V	T
S	T	R	E	A	M	X	Z	B	T	S	C	T

Fig. 12.5. Word Search—*Sun Up*.

Chapter 13—*Thunder Cake*

WORD LADDER ANSWERS— *THUNDER CAKE*

1.	Secret ingredient in thunder cake	tomato
2.	It accompanies thunder	lightning
3.	Another name for "grandmother"	babushka
4.	Place where animals are kept	barn
5.	Summer weather disturbances	thunderstorms
6.	Red fruit	strawberries
7.	Country where the grandmother was born	Russia
8.	State by the Great Lakes	Michigan
9.	Sound of thunder	kaboom
10.	Place where the granddaughter gathered eggs	Nellie Peck Hen
11.	Place where the granddaughter hid—under the _____	bed

```
            TOMATO
           LIGHTNING
           BABUSHKA
            BARN
          THUNDERSTORMS
      STRAWBERRIES
            RUSSIA


          MICHIGAN
           KABOOM
   NELLIE  PECK  HEN
            BED
```

Chapter 14—*Cloudy with a Chance of Meatballs*

WORD SCRAMBLE ANSWERS—WEATHER

a. gust

b. drift

c. tornado

d. wind

e. rain

f. hail

g. drizzle

h. snow

i. downpour

j. sleet

k. hurricane

l. shower

m. thunder

Chapter 15—*My Place in Space*

CROSSWORD ANSWERS—GALAXIES

Across

5.	Space beyond the limits of a celestial body (two words)	outer space
7.	Object that orbits a planet	moon
11.	Galaxy containing our planet (two words)	Milky Way
12.	All existing things	universe
13.	Instrument for studying celestial objects and bodies	telescope

Down

1.	Diffused mass of interstellar dust and gas	nebula
2.	Person who studies celestial objects and bodies	astronomer
3.	Celestial body with a tail and an elliptical orbit	comet
4.	Glowing ball of gas	star
6.	Grouping of galaxies	supercluster
8.	Distance light travels in one year (two words)	light year
9.	Celestial body illuminated by the star around which it orbits	planet
10.	Celestial objects that orbit the Sun; they may be fragments of a planet	asteroids

Chapter 16—*Berlioz the Bear*

WORD SCRAMBLE ANSWERS—ORCHESTRA INSTRUMENTS

Strings

a. violin

b. bass

c. viola

d. cello

Brass

e. trumpet

f. trombone

g. French horn

h. tuba

Woodwinds

i. oboe

j. clarinet

k. english horn

l. saxophone

Percussion

m. drums

n. piano

o. bells

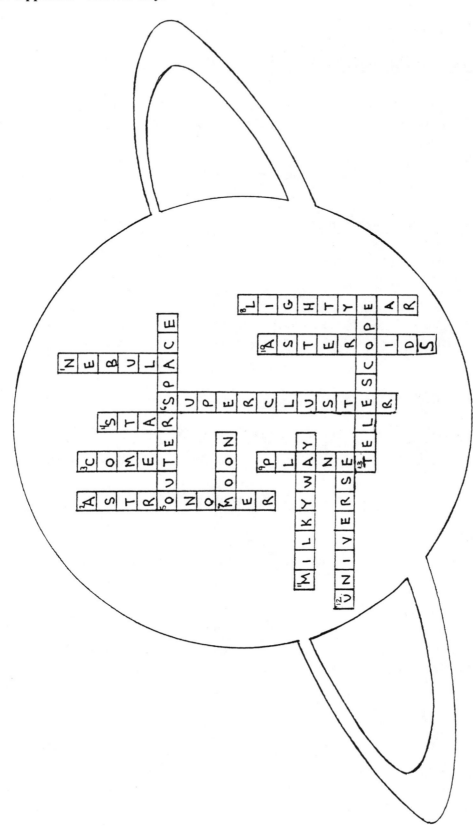

Fig. 15.5. Crossword—Galaxies.

Chapter 17—*The Ice Horse*

WORD MATCHING ANSWERS—SIMPLE MACHINES

Wheel and Axle
a. bicycle   b. wagon

Lever
c. baseball bat   d. crowbar

Wedge
e. ax   f. shovel

Inclined Plane
g. ramp   h. playground slide

Pulley
i. flagpole   j. window blind drawstring

Screw
k. corkscrew   l. auto jack

Chapter 18—*Ty's One Man Band*

The answer to the math puzzle is "My name is Andro. I'm a one man band."

Chapter 20—*The Sea-Breeze Hotel*

CROSSWORD ANSWERS—KITE FLYING

Across
2. Kites are often made in the form of this fierce creature   dragon
4. Kite with tension on one of the crosspieces   bow
5. Stay away from electrical _____ when flying a kite   wires
7. Keeps the kite connected to the person who flies the kite   string
8. Brothers who experimented with kites before they invented   Wright
    the airplane
10. Pyramid-shaped kite perfected by the man who invented the   tetrahedral
    telephone
13. In Asian countries, kite flying was often a part of the   religion
    _____ of the people
14. Helps give a kite its stability   tail
16. Kite Day is celebrated on the ninth day of the ninth month   China
    in this country
17. Keeps the kite up in the air   wind

Down
1. Square-shaped kite invented by Hargrave in Australia   box
3. *The Sea-Breeze Hotel* takes place in this country   Australia
4. Kites are often made in the form of this insect   butterfly

6. Kites are often flown to _____ oneself, to have fun   entertain
9. American who flew a kite to learn more about electricity   Franklin
11. Also known as a "plain" kite, it must have a tail to fly   flat
12. Usually an excellent month for flying kites   March
15. Asian country known for its delicate kites   Japan
16. Kites were used to _____ objects   carry

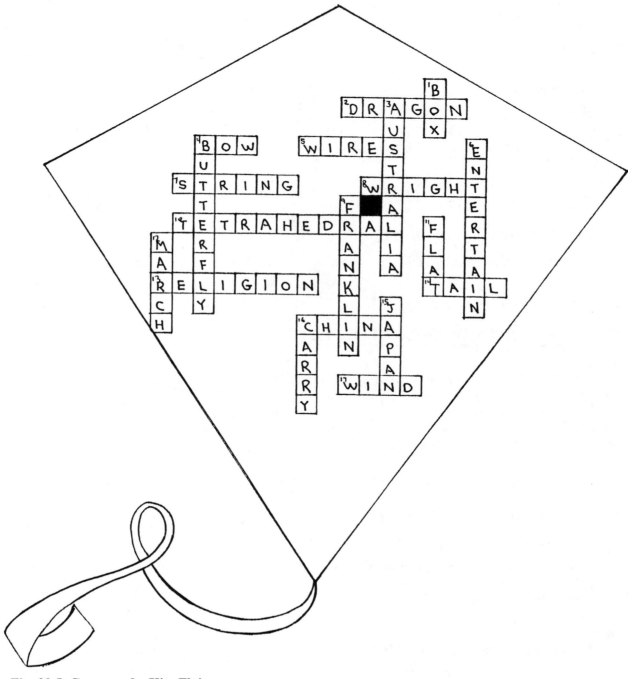

Fig. 20.5. Crossword—Kite Flying.

Chapter 21—*Plane Song*

WORD SEARCH ANSWERS— AIRPLANES

a.	Force that raises a plane	lift
b.	Speed of sound	Mach
c.	Body of an airplane	fuselage
d.	Building to house airplanes	hangar
e.	Strip of paved land for takeoffs and landings	runway
f.	Force of the Earth's pull	gravity
g.	On the inside of the wing; they help control downward movement	flaps
h.	One who travels between home and another city to work	commuter
i.	Mechanical implements for use in poor visibility	instruments
j.	Moveable control on an airplane wing; used for turning	ailerons
k.	Rear of the plane; includes the rudder	tail
l.	Force that slows a body in motion	drag
m.	Directed force	thrust
n.	Rotating blades that pull an aircraft forward	propeller
o.	Space for the pilot and crew	cockpit
p.	Wheels that touch the ground (two words)	landing gear
q.	Located on the tail; it helps steer the plane	rudder
r.	Freight carried by an airplane	cargo
s.	Airplane that does not use a propeller	jet
t.	Parts that provide lift and support	wings
u.	Place for airplane arrivals and departures	airport

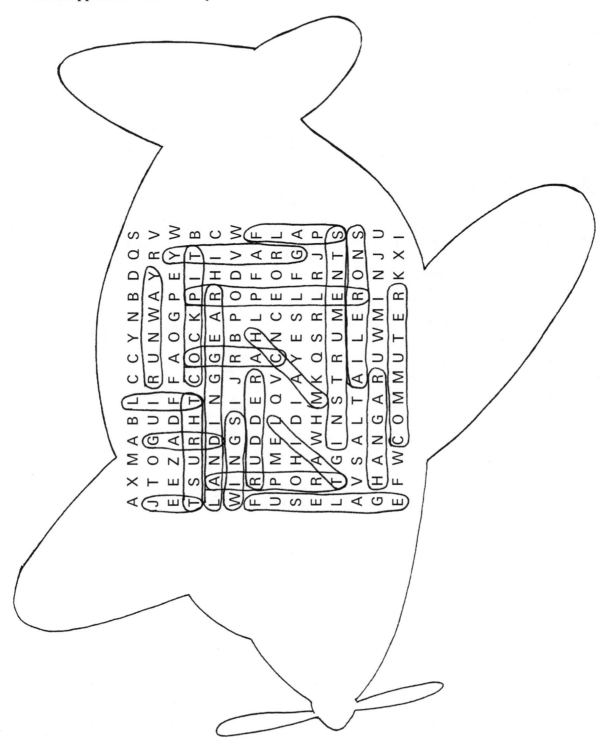

Fig. 21.11. Word Search—Airplanes.

Index

About the Authors

The Butzows live in Indiana, Pennsylvania, a small University town located in rural western Pennsylvania. One room of their home houses an extensive collection of children's and adolescent literature that provides the basis for the research involved in selecting books and developing instructional ideas included in their three books on the use of literature in elementary and middle school instruction.

Carol and John both have undergraduate degrees from St. Bonaventure University in New York State. In addition, Carol completed master's degrees in history from Colgate University and in reading education from the University of Maine. Carol's doctoral degree in elementary education was earned at Indiana University of Pennsylvania. John's master's degree was earned at St. Bonaventure, and his doctorate in science education came from the University of Rochester. Carol has many years of experience teaching at the middle-junior high level, as well as at the college level. John originally worked as a teacher of science and university science educator, and more recently has been a university administrator.

John and Carol h   d States,
including Alaska   d confer-
ences. They hav   **DATE DUE**   and, and
Sweden. For inf   ntations,
please contact th

	JUL 2 1 2003		
	JUL 1 5		
GAYLORD			PRINTED IN U.S.A.